In Your Opinion . . .

_In Your Opinion . . .

THE MANAGING EDITOR OF THE GALLUP POLL
LOOKS AT POLLS, POLITICS, AND THE
PEOPLE FROM 1945 TO 1960

by

John M. Fenton

WITH A FOREWORD
BY

DR. GEORGE GALLUP

LITTLE, BROWN AND COMPANY
BOSTON • TORONTO

Published simultaneously in Canada
by Little, Brown & Company (Canada) Limited

PRINTED IN THE UNITED STATES OF AMERICA

To Betty

Foreword

FOR TWENTY-FIVE YEARS, a systematic effort has been made to gauge American public opinion on the important issues confronting the nation.

This span of years — 1935 to 1960 — has bridged the end of a great depression, the anxious years before World War II, the war years, the uncertainty of reconversion, the beginning of the cold war and, most recently, a period of domestic prosperity and industrial expansion.

A unique opportunity has thus been presented to study the views of the American people under a wide variety of conditions and to arrive at conclusions on how the common people of the land react in times of stress as well as in times of complacency.

The beginnings of this effort to use scientific methods to report public opinion were described by Saul Rae and myself in *The Pulse of Democracy*. Public opinion in the prewar and war years was dealt with by William Lydgate in *What America Thinks*. The present volume by John Fenton rounds out the story of what public opinion polls have covered in the last quarter-century —

it concerns the fifteen eventful years which have followed the close of the Second World War.

No month has gone by in these twenty-five years when one or more nationwide Gallup Polls have not been conducted. Reports have appeared in the approximately one hundred newspapers which have supplied the funds for this continuing effort to measure and report the opinions of carefully drawn samples of the entire electorate. The editors of these papers have discovered that it is important to cover two kinds of news — news of *what people do* and news of *what people think*.

These surveys provide basic material for those students of democratic processes who wish to learn for themselves how well qualified the people are to deal with the great range of issues which confront a nation in the modern era.

Not only have the public's views been gauged on important political questions, but also, as this book shows, on the important social and economic problems of a period. From all of this experience in finding out what the public thinks, it is possible to see what function polls can and do serve in our type of democracy.

The fears entertained by some critics in the early days of scientific polling that these procedures would lead to *pure* democracy and subvert *representative* democracy have been allayed. So too have the fears of those who believed the polls would influence voters and create bandwagon movements. The record fails to present any evidence whatever that polls produce this effect.

On the contrary, poll findings have lent great comfort

to those who have faith in the common people. The collective judgment of our citizens has been found to be extraordinarily sound. The people, in fact, have been ahead of their elected representatives on a great number of the major issues of this period.

In the days when the Hitler menace began to assume frightening proportions, for example, the public saw the need to prepare for the possibility of our entrance into a Second World War. They anticipated before Congress did, or even the nation's military leaders, the vital role which air power would play in the coming war.

When war did come to the nation, the people were willing to make far greater sacrifices than the leaders actually called upon them to make. Commenting upon the public's views at this time, Robert Millikan, then president of California Institute of Technology, said in reviewing poll findings: "If all this does not show that the average American has more intelligence and more conscience than his political leaders, then I don't know straight thinking and straight social morals when I see them."

One of the many contributions made by public opinion polls has been to thwart the efforts of pressure groups on many occasions. When the spokesmen for these groups claim that they speak for millions of voters, their claims can now be challenged by polling data.

Polling organizations are, and should be, fact-finding institutions. Their responsibility ends with the objective reporting of survey results. Obviously they cannot be charged for the manner in which others may interpret or use poll findings. Nor can they be properly attacked for results which happen to be unpalatable to some people.

Just as barometers do not make the weather, but merely record it, so do modern polls *reflect,* but not *make* public opinion. This is a simple but basic distinction which some critics overlook.

Apart from showing what the public thinks, the public opinion polls have served the country in many other ways. The extent of the public's knowledge on any issue or problem can be ascertained quickly and accurately. Many enlightening facts about the habits and customs of the American people have also been collected by the public opinion polls.

With the establishment of polls in all of the leading democracies of the world, it is now possible to gather opinions on important issues swiftly and reliably and to compare the views of the people of one nation with those of another.

In the period of twenty-five years, polling has thus come to be accepted as part of the democratic process. Polls serve a useful function — Professor Samuel Stouffer of Harvard has said that they "represent the most useful instrument of democracy ever devised."

John Fenton is well qualified for the job of reviewing the trends of public opinion over the last decade and a half. He is experienced in scientific survey methods and is thoroughly familiar with political statistics. He has studied closely the voting habits of key groups and key areas where elections are won or lost. He has put in much time himself as a doorbell ringer, going directly to the only reliable source of political intentions in this country — the American voter. He uses this valuable background and experience in interpreting and presenting here the trends of public opinion and he does this objectively in the best traditions of journalism.

This book contributes to a quarter-century effort to chronicle the public's thinking. In telling the pollster's story of the past fifteen years, John Fenton takes a fresh and exciting look at the mind of the American electorate.

GEORGE GALLUP

Acknowledgments

MOST OF THE FACTS about the American people in this book come from public opinion sampling made by the Gallup Poll. Whenever other sources have been used, I have indicated this.

The conclusions drawn here are my own. But a number of others have helped in this account — most of all, perhaps, those voters who gave their opinions to the Gallup Poll and the reporters who collected them.

I would like to express my thanks to Dr. George Gallup for his counsel and advice throughout the writing of this book, as well as for originally encouraging me to undertake it.

I am grateful to Paul Perry, President of the Gallup Organization, for his careful reading of parts of the manuscript. Thanks are also due Emery Ruby, Executive Editor of the Gallup Poll, for general assistance and guidance.

Charles Roll of the Gallup Poll staff offered much help and support. So did George Gallup, Jr. — my teammate on a number of interviewing trips throughout the country during which many of the ideas for this book were first developed.

Dr. Hadley Cantril was kind enough to read and comment on the manuscript. And I am grateful for the editorial help I received from Alan Williams of Little, Brown and Company.

My thanks also to Mary Fenton, Mary Maher, Veronica Maher and Gloria Frohling for their help with the final manuscript.

Lastly, my heartfelt thanks to Betty Fenton, a wife who served continually and ably as a combination sounding board, editorial assistant and general morale booster.

J. M. F.

Contents

In Your Opinion . . .

1

Polls and People

IT HAS SOMEHOW ESCAPED the notice of historians, but it is a fairly sure bet that somewhere in the city of Harrisburg, Pennsylvania, on a morning in early 1825, at least one citizen awoke to the news of John Quincy Adams's surprise victory over Andrew Jackson and uttered that soul-satisfying phrase: "Those polls were wrong again."

The cause of his satisfaction would have been a July 24 report the previous year in the Harrisburg *Pennsylvania* of a "straw vote taken without discrimination of parties" which indicated Jackson to be the popular choice over Adams. As it turned out, Old Hickory was the popular choice in 1824 — in the election he ran ahead of Adams by more than fifty thousand votes. But he failed to get a majority of the electoral votes and the election was decided in the House of Representatives with the victory going ultimately to Adams on February 9, 1825.

This is by way of pointing out two things about public opinion polls.

First, what they attempt to do is often misinterpreted. Obviously, no poll of the people's choice could have foreseen Adams's victory — it was a matter out of the hands of the poll taker.

Second, in one form or another, the public opinion poll has been part of the American scene for well over one hundred years.

As a Gallup Poll editor, I have often seen instances where results of polls we have taken were misinterpreted by others. But I have rarely heard the acknowledgment that efforts to poll the public are not new. More often the polls are deplored as some kind of new-fangled device which somehow takes all of the fun out of the pre-election speculation.

Political party strategists have long used canvasses of voters during a campaign to help them determine how their candidate stands with the public. Politicians and pundits have never been loath to speculate about the possible behavior of this or that segment of the electorate. During the 1824 campaign, for example, a South Carolina Congressman, George McDuffie, sent out this stream of reports in letters to friends about his home state candidate, John C. Calhoun:

> Mr. Calhoun is rising rapidly in all quarters . . . New Jersey will give him an undivided vote . . . Calhoun is taking like wild fire in the western part of New York . . . the strongest indications are given that New England, believing that Mr. Adams cannot be elected, will support Mr. Calhoun.*

*Reported by Marquis James in his *Andrew Jackson, Portrait of a President.*

4

Three months after the last of these battle communiqués from Representative McDuffie, the Calhoun cause collapsed. The election of 1948 notwithstanding, the public opinion polls seem generally to have hit upon methods more accurate than those employed by Mr. McDuffie.

Being a Gallup Poll editor is a rewarding if sometimes overly responsible position. It is rewarding because in few other places can one work so closely with evidence that democracy can and does function adequately by relying on the generally sound judgment of the people. It sometimes seems overly responsible because you are dealing daily with the opinions of millions of your fellow Americans. The percentages on a pollster's tabulation sheet are the composite views of the American public. If I did not believe this was so, I could have little faith in the poll results which I am charged with interpreting.

Public opinion polls provide an invaluable source for the social historian seeking to analyze what was right or wrong with our age. Was Charles Van Doren's action on the TV quiz programs the symptom of a general American immorality? There is no precise answer, obviously. But a poll can find out that nearly three out of four Americans feel that most people would have done what Van Doren did. Another poll at the same time can reveal that less than 10 per cent of the American people believe honesty is a prime requisite for success.

How widespread was Senator Joseph McCarthy's popular support and where did he draw his greatest strength? What are our chief fears — real or imagined — about Communist Russia? What were some of the factors in

Eisenhower's phenomenal rise to national popularity? How many Northerners sympathize with the Southern segregationist? These are just a few of the important questions about the American people which public opinion polls can and do answer for the future student of United States history.

The public opinion poll has also dealt with many interesting sidelights on the American people and their thinking. The Gallup Poll has on file replies from more than two million Americans with whom its reporters have talked since the Poll's founding in 1935. A random check of these files turns up such information as . . .

Only about half of all Americans have ever eaten lobster . . . one person in seven in the United States has red hair . . . most American women would like to lose weight . . . most men in this country have no objection to their wives using mild profanity in public . . . only one American in five has ever gone hungry due to lack of money . . . gentlemen in the United States prefer brunettes to blondes . . . four out of ten Americans have climbed a mountain . . . over half of the public has had a drink of champagne.

The pollster's picture of America also shows that most wives think their husbands are handsome, that some five million Americans would volunteer to be the first person to go up in a space ship, that men don't like women to go on the street in Bermuda shorts, that more of us know that Mae West said "Come up and see me sometime" or that the Lone Ranger hollers "Hi yo, Silver" than know that Patrick Henry said "Give me liberty or give me death."

There have been a number of books about the public opinion polls — both on how they function and what they have found. A complete bibliography of the writing which reports poll findings would cover several pages. And there have been many excellent works of a more technical nature designed to aid the practitioner of survey sampling in various aspects of his job.

There have been few attempts since the end of World War II, however, to look at the broad picture of the American electorate which is provided by the polls. This is basically what I have tried to do — bringing together a number of poll findings on a wide range of topics, some purely political, others of a more general nature, and sometimes adding a dash of lighter poll results which help to bring out some of the flavor of an era. The end result is a kind of mosaic of Americans' thinking during the last fifteen years. It is, it seems to me, a new way of looking at our recent history. As Samuel Stouffer has said, poll results "open a window into the mind of America."

The 1824 straw vote shows that the public opinion poll is no first-generation American. In that same year, the Raleigh *Star* also undertook to canvass political sentiment at meetings in North Carolina "at which the sense of the people was taken." Throughout the nineteenth and into the early twentieth century, the chief sponsors of straw votes were the newspapers. Editors discovered that their readers were interested in the news of what people *think* as well as in the news of what people *do*. Some of the early leaders in this field were the *Boston Globe*, the *New York Herald*, the *Cincinnati Enquirer*, the *Columbus*

Dispatch, the *Chicago American,* and the *Chicago Record-Herald.* The efforts centered chiefly on attempting to forecast the outcome of elections; these early polls dealt only occasionally with issues.

The earliest of the magazine polls, the *Farm Journal,* was launched in 1912. In 1916, the *Literary Digest* made its first election forecast when it called the turn on Woodrow Wilson's re-election.

An explanation of why the *Literary Digest* went wrong in 1936 while the new-type polls conducted by George Gallup, Elmo Roper, Archibald Crossley and others were right shows clearly the differences between the early straw vote methods and the modern-day public opinion poll.

After twenty years of collecting straw votes, the *Literary Digest* had built an immense reputation (and also an immense circulation) on predicting presidential elections.* The total number of persons polled by the *Digest* was staggering by modern-day research standards — its final poll in 1936 was based upon a return of some 2,375,000 mail ballots. In August of that year, the *Digest* editorialized: "Like the outriders of a great army, the first ballots in the great 1936 Presidential campaign march into the open this week to be marshalled, checked and counted."

A month before this editorial appeared, the newly formed Gallup Poll (its first release appeared in October,

---

*The *Digest* clipped a subscription blank to each postcard ballot they sent out — a number which ran to nearly twenty million in 1932. In answering a 1924 charge of dishonesty, the *Digest* pointed out: "The returns in subscriptions have been enormous and they have paid the expense of the polls." The magazine had been accused of being in the pay of the Republicans.

1935) had warned its subscribing newspapers that the *Digest's* poll that year would point to the wrong man. Working from a sample of voters which approximated the characteristics of that used by the *Digest,* it estimated that the final totals of the poll would show about 56 per cent of the vote for the GOP nominee, Governor Alfred Landon. This proved to be one of the most accurate predictions the Gallup Poll ever made.* In November, the *Digest's* final report indicated that Landon would win with 57 per cent of the vote. The Kansas governor actually got 37.5 per cent of the vote, carried only two states, and the *Digest's* editors were faced with the job of explaining a colossal error of some 19 percentage points.

What spelled disaster for the *Digest* was a sample which did not reflect some sharp realignments which were occurring in the electorate during the first half of the 1930s. Their unbroken string of predictive successes from 1916 through 1932 took place in an era when Republicans and Democrats were distributed fairly evenly through all segments of the population. But the depression of the early '30s together with FDR's efforts to help the unemployed and other hard-hit segments of the electorate combined to divide the country politically more and more into the parties of the Haves and the Have Nots. The poorer

---

*It was a far more accurate prediction, incidentally, than that made by the Gallup Poll in estimating the 1936 vote. It has always struck me as ironical that the error made by the Poll in 1936 (6.8 percentage points) — a year which established the greater accuracy of the new-type polls — was actually greater than the error made in 1948 (4.8 percentage points). If a poll today were to have an error of the proportions of the one in 1936, it would be considered a near-disaster by most public opinion researchers.

9

working classes swung more heavily behind Roosevelt; the wealthier upper classes, disturbed by what appeared to them to be FDR's road to socialism, gravitated increasingly toward Landon and the Republican party.

The *Literary Digest*'s sample was drawn from lists of automobile owners and telephone subscribers. And two of the things that many Have Nots did not have in 1936 were cars and telephones. The sample, therefore, had a built-in bias in favor of the Haves — the people who tended to be more Republican.

The *Digest*'s 1936 failure emphasized the need to concentrate public opinion research on methods of getting the proper proportion of voters in all segments of the population, and not on interviewing vast numbers of people. Gallup, Roper and Crossley had operated on this theory in 1936 and all correctly picked the winner. The *Literary Digest*'s fault was not that they interviewed too few people — they interviewed fifty times as many people as a typical Gallup Poll did in 1936. The ratio today, with improvements in sampling, would be far greater.

The new methods used were based on the known scientific principles embodied in the *theory of probability*. The theory had been known to mathematicians for some three hundred years. Its development had been stimulated by problems involved in calculating the chances of a certain draw or throw in games of chances. It was not until this theory began to be applied to the "drawing" or selection of samples of *people*, however, that the modern-day public opinion poll was born. In effect, sampling statisticians took the same laws which can determine your chances of filling an inside straight and used them to determine what the chances are of drawing an accurate sample of the American public. They could then calculate fairly precisely just how far off they might be — that is, the extent to which a *sample* of the public's views might deviate from what would result if the total public had been interviewed.

When the pollster talks about his "margin of error," therefore, he means the extent to which his sample results might differ from a census of the adult population taken at the same time and asking the same question. In election polling, it means the extent to which the poll results might differ from the vote in what he calculates is the likely proportion of persons who will vote. With the Gallup Poll's present sample size, the chances are high that any poll result will be no more than a few percentage points away from the true figure. There is always the very slim chance, however, that a poll result will be farther away from actual public sentiment.

The new scientific polls in their formative stages, used methods which were crude by modern-day standards. The samples used were so-called *quota* or purposive samples in which the areas selected as interviewing locations were picked as being representative of a certain type of city, town or rural area. Within these areas, interviewers were instructed to select certain types of people who, in the interviewer's judgment, represented various groups within the population.

At the present time, most public opinion polls have come to use the *probability* sample design in their selection of interviewing areas. When areas are selected in this manner, the person doing the selecting has no knowledge beforehand about the specific cities or towns which will be drawn nor of the areas within these cities or towns from which voters will be selected. The sample of areas is, in effect, arrived at *by chance* — but it is a mathematical chance, and statisticians can therefore calculate just what the probabilities are that the sample is representative of the total country. Within the interviewing area, reporters work from prearranged selection codes in determining which people to question — they are allowed no personal choice in the matter. The total process is designed to minimize the bias which might be introduced either by the home-office statisticians or the interviewer in the field.

The practical application of these sampling theories can be seen in the procedures followed by the Gallup Poll in a national survey of public opinion.

There are about a thousand members on the Gallup Poll's national field staff. About seven out of ten are women. Most are engaged in some other full-time employment — there are schoolteachers, social workers, housewives, bank clerks, automobile salesmen, a photographer's model, a chiropractor and a professional hypnotist. A majority of the Gallup Poll interviewers have college educations; a recent count revealed nine with a Ph.D. degree.

On a regular national survey, between 150 and 180 of these opinion reporters receive assignments. The Gallup Poll tries to maintain from two to four interviewers in each sampling area in the event a sudden replacement is needed or a special survey arises in which a greater number of interviewers are called for in a certain region. Normally, interviewers are notified in advance that an assignment is coming; sometimes, however, a quick spot check of opinion allows time for no warning — the assignment comes by telephone from the home office. One interviewer recently was called to the phone from her evening bath at about ten o'clock. She accepted the assignment willingly (and wet); by 10:30 P.M. she was out questioning voters; by midnight she was phoning in her report to the home office; by one A.M. her report, along with the phone reports of other interviewers, was being compiled and tabulations were nearing completion.

With each regular assignment, the Gallup Poll interviewer receives a map on which is outlined the area to interview in. This is typically a city block or group of blocks, or, in rural areas, a segment of a township or county. Also indicated on the map are two "starting points." These starting points instruct the interviewer on where he commences two phases of his assignment — one in which he interviews only women, the other, only men. The starting points are generally located at a street corner, or the intersection of two country roads, or some other identifiable landmark which has been selected in the home office. Even this selection is not arbitrary — map division personnel follow a prearranged pattern on each survey. On every map, for example, they might pick out one starting point nearest the northwest corner of the interviewing area, the other nearest the southeast corner, or use some other consistent directional system.

At about three o'clock in the afternoon on weekdays, or at any hour on week ends, the Gallup Poll interviewer proceeds to his first starting point. From three until six he interviews only women. From six o'clock on, interviews are conducted from the second starting point and are made only with men. The division is made in order that men and women will be interviewed at hours when they are normally at home.

From each indicated starting point, the interviewer moves around the block in a clockwise direction and tries to obtain an interview at each household he contacts until he has completed that phase of his assignment.

Gallup Poll interviewers are instructed to skip the first house they pass after they leave the starting point. This is generally a corner house and, although it may come as a surprise to some people, there are still many towns in America where the corner house is occupied by a family of slightly better means. If interviews were made in every one of these corner houses, the national sample might be biased by including too many persons of affluence. A corner house encountered later in the interviewer's route is fair game; this falls naturally into the sample.

At each household in the first half of his assignment, the Gallup Poll interviewer asks to question the youngest woman who is at home who is twenty-one years of age or older. If the only woman at home is an eighty-year-old grandmother, she qualifies. If no women are at home, the interviewer moves on to the next doorbell. The same procedure is followed when working from the second starting point when only men are interviewed — the youngest man twenty-one or over is questioned.

This age selection plan is based on the known fact that the younger you are, the more chance there is that you will not be at home. By interviewing the young whenever they are encountered, an age distribution is obtained which closely parallels that recorded by the Census Bureau. If by some improbable chance one interviewer questioned all twenty-one-year-olds, it would not matter. This reporter would only be helping out another who might be encountering only eighty-year-old grandmothers and grandfathers in another area of the country. Actually, Americans tend toward homogeneity in their distribution by age across the country; most interviewers turn in completed assignments which include interviews from voters who are both young and old.

All of this is not just a statistical treasure hunt designed to confuse the interviewer (although occasionally it does). It serves to remove from the interviewer's hands the decision on where to start interviewing and whom to question, thus reducing the possibility of bias. If interviewers were given a choice in this matter, human nature might inevitably work to turn up a sample of front-porch sitters or, in rural areas, a representative scattering of farms without fierce-looking dogs.

When Gallup Poll interviewers complete their assignments, they mail their returns to the home office in Princeton, New Jersey. Answers are then analyzed and coded and the results of all questions are transcribed onto IBM cards. The sample of voters is then checked against the latest available Census data on the population.* The IBM cards are in turn run through electronic computers which count and then print the results. Analyses of the results, or breakdowns according to sex, age, occupation, political affiliation, geographic areas and dozens of other variables, are then compiled. The final figures and percentages are sent to the editorial staff, which works in collaboration with the Gallup Poll Director to prepare the public opinion news releases which are sent to subscribing newspapers. Over a hundred leading newspapers currently subscribe to the Gallup Poll service. They supply the sole financial support for the Poll. These newspapers represent every shade of political belief — Democratic, Republican, and Independent. It is a tribute to these papers and their editors that, despite wide differences in the policies advocated in their editorial columns, they have impartially reported the results of Gallup Poll surveys even when these conflicted violently with their own editorial opinions.

Probably the one question that readers ask most frequently about the Gallup Poll is: "Why haven't I been interviewed?" The answer is a matter of simple arithmetic. The Poll now samples the country's civilian adult population in units of 1500 voters. If this sample of 1500 persons were taken weekly, a total of 78,000 persons would be reached in a year. This would comprise less than one

---

*The latest available Census data is not, as it might sound, the information from the last decennial enumeration of the total population. The Census Bureau continually uses sampling methods to update the population findings obtained every ten years. Even in the 1960 Census, for example, the Census bureau "sampled" one out of four homes on certain questions.

tenth of 1 per cent of the total civilian adult population —
estimated in early 1960 at about 105,000,000 persons.

If, by chance, you have been interviewed by the Gallup
Poll, you were speaking, in effect, for about 69,000 of your
fellow American voters. Obviously your opinions on a
given issue are not necessarily the same as those held by
this many voters. But you do share many things with at
least 69,000 of your fellow citizens — maybe it is the fact
that you went to college, or are in your thirties, or work
at a certain type of job. The very act of your reading a
book, in fact, would give you one characteristic in common with many millions of Americans on any day in the
week.

On a typical Gallup Poll questionnaire, each person is
asked in the vicinity of 35 to 40 questions. The subject
matter will range from the President's popularity to political preferences to Russia's latest international move to
Dior's latest move in the world of fashion. Many questions are included chiefly to help to analyze a voter's
opinion on one key issue. In the fall of 1959, for example,
voters were asked not only if they approved or disapproved of Premier Khrushchev's visit to the United States
but why they felt the way they did, what they thought
Khrushchev had come to see, how they felt people would
welcome the Russian leader and what they personally
would like to ask Khrushchev if they had a chance to
meet him. All these questions were helpful in interpreting
just what lay behind a voter's general approval or disapproval of the visit.

In questions asked in a modern public opinion poll, the

wording is simple and the question is generally short. The tone must be kept as neutral as possible. This is all by way of avoiding what can be one of the pollster's greatest pitfalls — the so-called loaded question.

Sometimes just the act of bringing up a question loads it. As Stanley Payne notes in *The Art of Asking Questions,* the poet's question "And what is so rare as a day in June?" is actually loaded. A statistician could point out that exactly ninety days are as rare as a June day — namely any day in April, September or November — and that, statistically speaking, a day in February is even rarer. But as Payne says, "we let the poet get away with his presumptuous question and probably nod our agreement as we read on."

A pollster if he wished, could deliberately load a question — and sometimes he is forced to do just that. For example, if you wanted to find out from a friend on Election Day if he had been to the polls, you would probably ask him: "Have you voted?" or, even worse, "Have you voted yet?" Either form, especially the second, implies that he naturally *should* vote. To measure voting participation, the pollster has to resort to the awkward phrasing: "In the election did things come up which kept you from voting, or did you happen to vote?" Americans don't like to admit they didn't vote; even this question always nets a few who say they voted and actually didn't — pollsters have to adjust for this tendency.

By suggesting endorsement from a source which the voter respects, a question can also be loaded. If you say President Eisenhower wants such-and-such an action, some voters will agree with the action simply because they feel that "Ike knows best," and not necessarily because they have thought the issue through themselves. If, on the other hand, you say Khrushchev or Russia wants the same action, some voters may veto the idea because they distrust anything suggested by the Soviet Union. You would be far safer to ask straight out, "Do you approve or disapprove of [this action]?"

No matter how carefully the question is pretested, however, most questions will encounter a few persons who do not understand the issue. Rather than forcing an answer under these circumstances, most questions allow the voter the opportunity of stating that he has no opinion.

Generally speaking, there are three types of No Opinion voters. They might be described broadly as the *uncomprehending*, the *uninterested* and the *undecided*. The first are those just mentioned — persons who do not comprehend the issue as it is stated. Pollsters try to reduce their number by various means. They may use a so-called "filter" question which filters out beforehand those who do not understand the issue. All voters may be first asked if they have heard or read anything about an issue. Those who say they have may then be asked to explain in their own words just what is their understanding of the issue. Or they may be asked some specific information questions about other aspects of the issue. These go on the assumption that if a person has such information, he is probably well enough informed about the central issue to give an opinion.

The second type of No Opinion voter may fully understand the question, but just not be interested in the issue. One woman who fell somewhere in between these two types of No Opinion voters was questioned recently by a Gallup Poll reporter who was seeking the public's view on whether or not the United States should stop testing hydrogen bombs. The lady was hard of hearing. After the interviewer had practically shouted the question to her, she thought a moment, then replied: "Well, I'm kind of deaf, you know, and I can't hear those bombs go off. So it doesn't really make much difference to me one way or the other." Everyone, it seems, has his reason for not being interested in a certain issue.

The third kind of voter in the No Opinion column is the one who is fully informed on the issue, may have much interest in it, but who has not been able to make up his mind one way or the other. In an election poll, for example, there are always some people who don't know how they are going to vote until they actually get in the booth.

Even our better-informed citizens are sometimes unable to take a stand pro or con on an issue. The Gallup Poll has on occasion sampled the views of persons listed in *Who's Who in America*. These polls of the nation's opinion leaders invariably turn up a certain number in the No Opinion category, who are honestly unable to categorize their views as being either for or against some issue.

Just what proportion of the total No Opinion vote each category makes up is impossible to judge precisely. It seems likely, however, that it is reserved largely for the *uninterested*. The *uncomprehending* we try to reduce by other question devices or by keeping the question itself short and simple. The *undecided* vote is probably small because public opinion poll questions generally deal with broad, basic issues which are very much in the news. And the chances of your being a No Opinion voter tend to relate very closely to the amount of formal education you have had — the more you have, the more chance there is you will have an opinion either pro or con.

The No Opinion voter is in a sense a creation of the public opinion polls. As Gallup points out in *A Guide to Public Opinion Polls,* "it was an issue which did not arise during the straw vote or post card poll era for the very simple reason that the people who returned their cards were the ones who had an opinion, or they were given no opportunity by the conductor of the straw poll to vote other than 'Yes' or 'No.' "

It is of course important to know how many of our citizens do not have an opinion on an issue. But some have reasoned that the No Opinion voter does not really represent a part of public opinion. And it is true that there is really no way to vote "No Opinion" in an election — except perhaps by not voting at all. In a democracy, public opinion is directly expressed by the vote. What counts, by and large, is not how many stayed away from the polls, but which man gets the most votes.

The aspect of opinion polling which seems to create the most interest is the so-called forecast of an election by the public opinion pollsters. And it often seems to the practitioner of public opinion research that the 1948 forecast on the *wrong* side is better remembered than almost any other fact about the public opinion polls. (What went wrong in 1948, incidentally, is discussed later in this book.)

Pre-election tests of political sentiment are important. But this is not because they tell people what is going to happen before it actually does. Strictly speaking, polls do not *forecast* political behavior — although the word has come into popular usage to describe a poll's final estimate of voting sentiment. What they actually do, throughout the campaign, is attempt to measure and report the situation at a given point.

Pre-election polling serves primarily two purposes. One helps the pollster himself. The other can aid the candidate whose chances are being tested by the poll.

Estimating the outcome of an election permits public opinion researchers to put their methods to an exacting test. Results obtained by the sampling method can be judged in the light of actual election results and can be compared down to the last decimal point. Elections are, in effect, the laboratories in which polling methods are tested. In each election new problems in polling come to light and procedures are developed to overcome them. In the first election covered by the Gallup Poll, it correctly picked Roosevelt to win, but the final estimate of his vote was 7 percentage points away from what he actually got. In the latest election covered, the 1958 Congressional election, the final estimate of the vote was one half of 1 percentage point off.

The chief benefit that a political candidate derives from pre-election polling is that it gives him an impartial and accurate appraisal of where he stands at various stages of the campaign. Poll results can serve as a kind of radar-scope on which political strategists can plot their next moves. A candidate who is ahead in the polls should not interpret this as meaning he is in safe. The polls should be read as indicators as to where he must work harder or how new campaign battle lines should be drawn. They cannot predict how many votes he will get by a series of hard-hitting speeches; they can suggest where these speeches might do him the most good and what they might deal with. Dr. Henry Durant, Director of the British Gallup Poll, suggests how election polls should be used: "Recon-naisance is as important in the art of politics as it is in the art of war — or the art of love."

The public opinion polls have seen their share of critics down through the years. From the apocryphal gentleman in Harrisburg in 1824 up to the present day, many have questioned poll findings and polling methods. One attack on the Gallup Poll came in late 1939 when the editors of *American Progress*, a journal friendly to the cause of the Huey Long machine, took exception — in rich prose — to the Poll's finding that Earl Long (the recently retired Governor of Louisiana) was trailing Sam Jones in the gubernatorial campaign that year:

> Three months ago a half dozen post graduate "Social Science Workers" from Princeton University, augmented by seven or eight East Side New Yorkers who had never in their lives seen a possum, tasted a sweet potato or chewed a plug of tobacco, arrived in New Orleans to conduct a so-called "survey of public opinion."

23

After taking a few sight-seeing trips, getting some fancy grub at the famous restaurants in New Orleans, looking at some swamps and sending picture post cards back home they then wrote some mystic figures in their little black books and hurried back to their boss, a low-ceiling guy with bifocal glasses who sits enthroned way up there in Princeton, New Jersey, like the Wizard of Oz and peers owlishly at figures all day long until he looks like a left handed figure "4."

And out of this hocus-pocus of numbers and dope sheets and form charts, lo and behold, if up didn't jump the Gallup Poll!

In the actual election two months later, to the chagrin of the editors of the *Progress,* the Long machine was ousted and Sam Jones became governor.

While in line of duty for the Gallup Poll, I have traveled maybe fifty thousand miles in all, crisscrossing this country to get the people's opinion. Assignments to interview special groups of voters on such diverse topics as segregation, McCarthyism, the farm problem and the use of leisure time have given me an unparalleled opportunity to meet the people. It has meant, at times, trying to outwit the doorman who didn't want to let you ring apartment doorbells in New York City's East Sixties. Or convincing an Iowa farmer that you have no connection with Mr. Benson's Department of Agriculture. Or even in making clear to the lady in the negligee who peeks from behind her door that your intentions are honest. To an overwhelming degree, I have found that the people are friendly and eager to state their opinions.

Gallup Polls have been conducted under every conceivable circumstance — shouted through a closed door by a voter who was taking a bath, taken at the top of a ladder on which interviewer and interviewee were balanced precariously, held in a rowboat bobbing in a Mississippi flood. One interviewer spent a night in jail. Another returned for one more try at a man who had refused to be interviewed and found that he had been murdered in the interim. One Gallup Poll interviewer regularly packs his sleeping bag for a three-day trip by jeep into the rugged Grand Canyon area to get the opinions of Indians in their hogans; another's assignment brought her to the New York apartment of Mrs. Eleanor Roosevelt. In the course of their assignments, Gallup Poll interviewers have killed rattlesnakes, helped to deliver babies, prevented suicides and sobered drunks.

During the course of one interviewing trip, the Gallup Poll's Director was asked by a woman he was questioning just how the Gallup Poll worked. He explained that basically it involved doing exactly what he was doing at the moment — asking voters for their opinions. To which she commented: "Well you know, Dr. Gallup, I always thought you did it with statistics."

In a way it is true that at the Gallup Poll we do it with statistics. But they are statistics gained from the people — they represent the collective emotions, fears, hopes and desires of the American public. They are the raw material out of which is created public opinion — that force which has intrigued politicians, philosophers and poets down through the ages.

In a democracy, most responsible leaders give some attention to public opinion. A sudden flood of Congressional mail, even if obviously triggered by a pressure group, will cause at least some of our elected representatives to react. Leaders have given some heed to the voice of the people for centuries regardless of the form of government they headed. Wendell Willkie pointed out in *One World*: "Even Stalin had his form of 'Gallup Poll,' and it is recorded that Napoleon at the height of his power, as he sat astride his white horse amid the smoldering ruins of Moscow, anxiously waited for his daily courier's report of what the mobs in Paris were thinking."

In the years since World War II, the United States has come to hold a position of moral and ideological leadership throughout much of the free world. This places an awesome responsibility in the hands of those who, in the final analysis, control the destinies of this democracy and its leaders — the American voters. It is obviously important to have an impartial, accurate and swift appraisal of just what these voters are thinking. In attempting to provide such an appraisal the public opinion polls have contributed to the cause of democracy. This chapter has tried to suggest some of the methods used by the public opinion polls in making this appraisal. The chapters that follow attempt to report just what this appraisal has shown in the last fifteen years.

Some preliminary comments about reporting polling results may be useful. It should be pointed out, for example, that Americans are almost never 100 per cent for or against anything. Generally speaking, when the vote on any proposition divides 60 per cent in favor, 40 per cent opposed, the majority can be considered substantial. When Eisenhower won in 1956 with 58 per cent of the popular vote, it was widely interpreted as a huge landslide. When 70 or 80 per cent of the people are for or against anything, it is not only unusual but indicative of a rare degree of agreement among a people so diverse in their cultural and economic backgrounds.

The Gallup Poll preserves verbatim comments from certain individual voters which seem to typify general reactions to a given issue. From time to time I have drawn on these comments; other comments I have heard personally while in the course of interviewing voters.

Mainly I have reported the poll findings either as percentages or by saying that three out of four, two out of three, and so on were behind a given issue. At times, however, it has seemed more meaningful to talk about so many millions of Americans doing this or that. Since the Gallup Poll samples the national adult civilian population, it is possible to project poll findings in terms of actual millions in the population.

Since this is essentially the story of the total American public, I have generally reported only the overall results obtained by national polls. I report breakdowns by various groups in the population only where these breakdowns help to interpret public opinion or where interest obviously centers on one region or one group in the population.

2

When War Ends and Peace Starts

ONLY TWO TOP HATS were in evidence among the distinguished guests attending Roosevelt's fourth inauguration — one worn by Georgie Jessel, the other by the Governor of New Hampshire. The abbreviated wartime ceremony on the south portico of the White House on January 20, 1945, was austere and solemn. One of the smallest gatherings ever to witness such an occasion stood quietly and listened to the President, bareheaded and without an outside coat despite the raw weather, take the oath of office and then deliver a carefully enunciated and unusually slow-spoken address of some five hundred words. Only those up on the portico could see how agonizing it was for Roosevelt to rise to take the oath following the swearing in of Harry S. Truman as Vice-President.

An administration without parallel in United States history had but eighty-two days to run. By the early spring of 1945, the sudden death of Roosevelt placed the reins of government in the hands of the relatively unknown former Senator from Missouri. In a Gallup Poll taken one week after the inauguration, one American in three could not tell you who the new Vice-President was.

The news from the battlefronts was reassuring in late January. The American First Army, recovered from the setback at the Bulge, was gaining ground slowly along the German border. Our Russian allies were rolling a hundred miles west of Warsaw, only two hundred miles from Berlin. In the Pacific, MacArthur's Sixth Army on Luzon had cut the Japanese forces in two.

The American public had long been confident that the nation and its allies would ultimately defeat the Axis powers. As early as 1938, 86 persons in every 100 in a Gallup Poll believed that England and France would defeat Germany if war came. The public's confidence

CONFIDENCE IN ALLIED VICTORY
Percentage Saying Allies Would Win

September, 1938	86
May, 1939	83
August	92
October	90
May, 1940	65
Early June	49
Late June	48
July	63
September	79
May, 1941	72
*December	96
July, 1942	93

* After Pearl Harbor

29

waned during the early dark days of 1940, but during only one brief period — in the weeks after Dunkirk — did the Gallup Poll find that those who expected the Nazis to win outnumbered those who expected the Allies to win. Once the United States entered the war, belief in victory rose sharply to a point where there was overwhelming confidence in an Allied triumph. By early 1945, fewer than one American in ten said there was even any *chance* of our losing the European conflict. Our guess then on when the Nazis would be defeated placed the end of the European war, at that time, somewhere in midsummer of 1945.

There were, of course, minor irritations — the most vexing "little thing" about the war was the shortages. The hardest thing to do without, we said, was butter (it was served at the White House only once a day). We also missed sugar and those prime cuts of beef, steaks and other meats. We were put out least by the shortage of gasoline — the age of America on wheels was to come after the war.

Very few of us were particularly bothered by the midnight entertainment curfew imposed early in 1945. A Gallup Poll found that 95 per cent of Americans were normally in bed before the curfew hour — only 5 per cent were up after midnight on a typical night.

The thriving business done by the black market during the war could be explained in part by the belief of one American in five that buying on the black market was *sometimes* justified — chiefly, however, "only when you really need things."

The public was the first to confess that the war had not meant much real suffering — two out of three Americans said they could not think of one real sacrifice they had made during the war. A clear majority (57 per cent) said it was willing to put up with shortages of butter, sugar and meat in order to help feed the starving millions in Europe. We said we could eat one-fifth less food each day to help provide these needed supplies and would go along with this reduction for as long as two years after the war if necessary.

There is no calculating, of course, the anguish that many millions had gone through worrying about sons, fathers, brothers and friends in the armed services. A farmer from the little town of Homer, Louisiana, summed up his sacrifice to a Gallup Poll reporter: "I've sent six boys off to the war." For hundreds of thousands of families, the sacrifice was a tragedy spelled out in the government phrase: "The War Department regrets to inform you." Nearly half a million Americans in the services lost their lives during the three and a half years of our participation in the war; well over half a million more were wounded. At war's end, a poll showed that the Purple Heart medal was as familiar to Americans as was the veteran's "Ruptured Duck."

But in a purely material sense, a great many Americans were not hard hit by the war shortages. Complaints over the shortage of sugar came in a year when our consumption of candy averaged about eighteen pounds per person. The typical American home in February, 1945, was heated to a comfortable 70 degrees. Seven out of ten persons in a Gallup Poll at that time said they had milk to drink at their last meal, three in ten had cheese, more than one in ten had ice cream. Nearly half of all Americans, a year after the war was over, could say that their life had not been changed greatly by the war.

Our certainty about winning the war was matched only by our confidence in winning the peace. In the flush of a fast-approaching victory over Germany, hope in our new allies and new war-created organizations soared. A majority viewed the accomplishments of the Big Three meeting at Yalta with optimism, believing that there had been general agreement reached on the conduct of the war and the maintenance of peace.

As American and Red Army troops drove toward the Elbe, the belief that the Russians would cooperate with us after the war was never higher. The public thought a military alliance with the Russians might be a good idea after the war. With the San Francisco conference coming up that April, our approval of the United Nations was never greater — either before or since that time. Most Americans could foresee no war ahead for at least twenty-five years. As the final surrender became a matter of days, our excitement in the onrush of events made us a little giddy perhaps, a little inclined to see anything and everything in a hopeful light.

In the state of shock following President Roosevelt's death, we gave President Truman an overwhelmingly high vote of confidence after his performance in office for what was really a short time (six weeks) in which to judge his executive ability. A total of 87 per cent of the public, in the first Gallup Poll check on Truman's popularity, said they approved of the way he was handling his job. Only three Americans in a hundred could find reason to disapprove of Mr. Truman at that time; even more surprising, only ten in a hundred felt themselves incapable of judging on the evidence they had. A comparable degree of unanimity was never recorded for Roosevelt or for Eisenhower. Just one year later, those disapproving of Truman's performance in office outweighed those approving. The closest he got to that record high again (once the initial honeymoon was over) was 69 per cent approval in January, 1949.

Optimism about the economic outlook in the postwar world was high. A great many Americans were confident that they would continue to make as much, if not more, money than they were making in that era of fat overtime salaries. Two out of three Americans believed that there would be from five to seven years of prosperity following the cessation of hostilities in Europe and the Pacific.

Our thoughts on keeping the peace centered more on the immediate problem of dealing with Nazism than they did on the long-range outlook. We wanted to disarm Germany permanently, deal with the enemy's leaders harshly and impress upon the German people the horror of what their leaders had done.

Just how harsh we wanted to be can be seen in various poll findings near the end of the war. Two out of three Americans voted death for Hermann Goering, with a number advocating torture before the execution. Nearly half of those interviewed in another Gallup Poll wanted to kill all Gestapo and SS members — with slow death recommended by some persons. Only about half wanted Hitler executed — either quickly or by slow torture. But another one in five felt death was too kind for the Nazi leader — they suggested torture without the mercy of death or caging him and sending him on exhibition around the world. Nine out of ten believed that the German people should be shown the atrocity films taken in concentration camps. One American in eight wanted Germany reduced to a completely agricultural state.

The problems of dealing with Germany, however, were not all so grim. When the question of GIs fraternizing with German girls arose, America's women vetoed the idea by a big majority — with younger women the most opposed. America's men, although opposed, were by no means as certain that it was a bad idea — with younger men most likely to feel that fraternizing wtih the Fräuleins was all right.

Much more important than worrying about the problems of a lasting peace, as far as the public was concerned, was the question of providing economic security here at home. Our optimism about the economic outlook was tempered by a certain uneasiness. When asked what would be the biggest postwar problem the United States would have to face, only 5 per cent of Americans named keeping the peace; 71 per cent cited some problem relating to personal financial security.

Just how to achieve this security and keep everybody happy was a debatable point. Our thinking on the ideal postwar world — as revealed in various surveys — is a study in contradiction. Most of us wanted things after the war to be pretty much as they had been before it started — or at least as we remembered them. Mark Sullivan's description in *Our Times* of the mood in 1920 provides an interesting comparison:

> Of all the nostalgic longing for the past that man has experienced since theology first taught him to look back toward Eden, hardly any was greater than the homesickness with which much of the world in 1920 looked back toward the world of 1914, in vain. That homesickness was responsible for many of the votes that Warren G. Harding got when he ran for President of the U.S. in 1920; of all the speeches he made in his campaign, the three words that most appealed to the mood of the country, the one phrase for which he was most applauded, was "back to normalcy."

Our desire for "normalcy" in 1945 was a desire to return to the forty-hour week. Yet this was contradicted by our expectations of making more money. Hopes of an America just the way it used to be ran head on into the plans of some 15 million Americans to build a new home after the war (on which they planned to spend an average of $5000). We hoped that the postwar cars would not differ substantially from those built before the war (a finding in a *New York Herald Tribune* study). But many Americans — an estimated 60 million — wanted to travel more after the war (and obviously in the latest comfort).

Certainly no American wanted to return to the depression conditions of the prewar world. There were eight million unemployed in one month in 1940. People averaged

66 cents an hour for their labor. What Americans seemed to be voting for in 1945 was the comfortable familiarity of the past when faced with the perplexing uncertainty of the future.

A $5000 home was the kind of home that *was* possible — although out of range for most — in 1938. A car just like the new one you bought in 1940 — and had to make do with all during the war — would be a symbolic reassurance that peacetime was here again.

It probably didn't help our state of mind much that the end of the war came so quickly, nor that it was brought about because of a new and awesome weapon — the atomic bomb. We had expected the war against Japan to last, on the average, about a year longer than it did. We believed that the Japanese were a lot more likely to fight it out to the bitter end than the Germans.

News of the atomic bomb on Hiroshima hit the American public as did few other single events in the war. Only a few days after it was dropped, a phenomenally high number (96 per cent) had heard about the new weapon. Approval of our having used it was then widespread (85 per cent nationwide) in all parts of the country and throughout all levels of American society.

But if the bomb meant the arrival of peace, it also meant the beginning of the postwar world — two things that we placed conveniently, if illogically, in separate categories. Suddenly, without any real warning, we were handed up the job of reconversion by an infernal machine which almost nobody even vaguely understood. The mushroom cloud over the Japanese cities meant we were planted squarely in peacetime; it even gave this new age the name of the Atomic Era.

The very weapon with which we had ended the war soon rose to plague us. As early as October — only two months after most Americans first heard about the atomic bomb — one person in three in a survey said he wished it had never been invented.

The epidemic of strikes in the war's aftermath could be directly tied to American concern with the economic situation. The labor stoppages were based mainly on the union demand that wages be raised to maintain the workers' take-home pay at the level of wartime wages — when overtime was a standard feature of most war workers' pay checks. We had gotten used to some pretty high living during the war years and were not about to stop it. A total of 3.5 million workers were involved in strikes during 1945 — most of them in the latter half of the year. There were nearly five thousand strikes in all. Some 38 million man days were involved.

The higher wages during the war had meant an inevitable rise in the prices of consumer goods. With war work overtime no longer coming in, the American workingman asked for a higher base pay to cope with price increases such as these between 1942 and 1946:

	1942	1946
Washing machine	$91.00	$112.00
Electric iron	4.34	8.64
Refrigerator	155.00	207.00

If the postwar era had its share of problems, it also had a healthy measure of exciting progress and growth for the nation. It was an era that the typical American entered cautiously, with a natural question mark in his mind about each new and unfamiliar item — jet planes, DDT, television, anti-knock motor fuel, and plastic food containers. The years immediately following the war saw great material expansion. There were more homes, more cars, more appliances, more of just about everything — above all, more people.

A Gallup Poll finding on the ideal family size heralded the population explosion that was to come. In 1941, about one woman in five between the ages of 21 and 34 felt four children was the ideal number in a family. By 1945, nearly one woman in three in this age group believed four children was the ideal number for a family to have. During the same period, the percentage of young women who would limit the family to just two children dropped sharply — from 40 per cent down to 25 per cent.

During the war years, due to the millions of military personnel sent abroad, the civilian population had remained fairly constant, changing less than a million overall. In the five years following the war, the population swelled by 18 million. Four million babies were born in the first year after the war.

The move to urban America — in evidence since about 1900 — continued once the war was over. Between 1945 and 1950, metropolitan areas grew twice as fast as rural areas. Before the war, the migration had been into the big city proper. Now millions were moving into the areas around the cities — filling, and in many instances creating, the suburban outskirts.

To supply the wants of this new suburban society, we needed new kinds of workers — specialists who could assemble prefabricated homes, repair television sets and new kitchen appliances, build new roads with earth movers developed by the military engineers during the war.

At the end of the war, seven out of ten Americans, a Gallup Poll found, had never been up in an airplane of any kind; only one in fourteen had ever flown with a regularly scheduled airline. Given our choice of the best way to take a thousand-mile trip, the railways won out handily over the airways. About 20 million adults in 1945 had braved a plane flight; by 1954 an estimated 42 million of us had been up in a plane. By 1950 — according to the Census Bureau — there were three times as many airplane pilots and navigators as there had been in 1940. In 1959 alone, commercial airlines flew passengers an estimated total of about 35 million miles.

Other changes in the occupational breakdown compiled by the Census Bureau present a revealing picture of the changing society in the first few years after World War II. Between 1940 and 1950, the number of industrial engineers tripled. By 1950, there were twice as many road equipment operators as in 1940. The number of plasterers, plumbers, roofers and carpenters also doubled in that decade — with most of the increase coming in the five years from 1945 to 1950.

Still another Census Bureau statistic tells an additional aspect of the postwar world. There were five times as many persons in public administration in 1950 as in 1940. And there was a great increase in the number of Americans engaged in producing paper during this same decade.

Meanwhile, decreasing in the United States labor force were bill collectors, telegraph messengers, tailors, maids, laundresses, milliners and boardinghouse operators. Credit cards, extension telephones, wash-and-wear fabrics, laundromats, and housing developments were replacing them.

From a political point of view, the end of the war found an electorate which had come through a period of both physical and mental uprooting. In a purely physical sense, World War II sent millions of Americans away from their homes and communities for unnaturally long periods of time. At the time of the Normandy invasion, nearly seven and a half million Americans were out of the country on duty with the armed forces. A total of 15 million persons served in the military forces in the war — about one adult in every six was away from his home, family and normal voting place during considerable periods of time between 1941 and 1945.

Here at home, many millions more were on the move. Few people in the world are so mobile as the American people. It is estimated that only two or three persons in every hundred in this country spend their entire lives in the house in which they were born. From 1935 through 1940, about six out of ten families were classed as "non-mobile" by the Census Bureau — meaning they did not change their place of residence during that period. But from 1940 through 1947, well over half of the population was in the "mobile" classification.

One election statistic tells of the kind of impact that this mobility had on the political scene. The 1942 Congressional elections saw one of the lowest vote turnouts in a national election in recent history. Only about 33 per cent of persons eligible to vote actually got to the polls, far below the normal turnout in an off-year election.

The war had set in motion two other forces which have had an important impact on American politics since 1945. The first of these was the spirit of bipartisanship which came to mark the electorate's attitude toward the fight against fascism. The second was the elimination of isolationism as a truly potent force in American public thinking.

It is an American political tradition that politics stops at the water's edge. Once we were committed in the fight against fascism, public opinion polls noted little real quarrel between Democrats and Republicans over the merits of the struggle. What differences there were grew chiefly out of varying opinions on how we could best conduct the war effort.

This kind of unanimity has been kept alive in the years since World War II by the cold war. It is hard now to find a really important anti-Russia issue on which Republicans and Democrats do not see virtually eye to eye. Again it is not a question of *whether* we should take a firm stand against international Communism, but one of *how* and *with what* we should fight the ideological battle. The one major political movement since the war which advocated any degree of accommodation with Russia — Henry Wallace's Progressive Party of 1948 — failed to enlist his supporters wholeheartedly in the new approach to Russia for which Wallace campaigned.

41

This bipartisanship has characterized the approach of our Congressional leaders. In his study of parliamentary attitudes in seven leading democracies, *Six Allies and a Neutral*, Lloyd Free makes the following comment about bipartisanship in the United States legislative branch:

> Obviously, *both* political parties in the United States must be classified as Center parties. The U.S. is the exception in having no leftist party, which accounts very largely for the high degree of American unanimity on foreign policy issues.

The decrease of isolationism as a widespread political doctrine in the United States had also obviously played a role in the creation of this bipartisanship. It removed from the political arena one more argument with which a party's candidate could previously sway a considerable number of voters.

In a 1935 Gallup Poll, seven out of ten persons were opposed to the United States joining with other nations to help stop aggression by one country against another. Until almost the very day the Japanese attacked Pearl Harbor, large majorities in this country were against the United States getting into either the European or Asian war. From December 7, 1941, majorities equally as large endorsed our going to war against both Japan and Germany. Although pockets of isolationism still remain, this political philosophy has ceased to have enough voter appeal to warrant the consideration of a major party's candidate in a national campaign.

The general growth of a bipartisan internationalism in

the voters' outlook on foreign policy has served to decrease the interest which might be engendered in the electorate by sharply contrasting political views on how to deal with the U.S.S.R. In a world where rival camps both possess the ultimate weapons of destruction, it is no longer possible to run for office on a variation of "Fifty-four-forty or fight."

The end of the war found the American people on the eve of a period of tremendous material expansion. It was a period faced with great uncertainty — an uncertainty born of the war, which would show in some of our reactions to the problems which shortly arose. The whims of history gave this period to Harry S. Truman to see what he could do with it.

3

Harry S. Truman

Man Riding a Tiger

JUST A FEW HOURS after Harry S. Truman was sworn in as
Vice-President, he received this telegram from five of his
former farmer neighbors in Jackson County, Missouri:
"Dear Harry. When you came home from World War I
to the home farm, you sold your mules and saddle horses.
We all knew you were going somewhere. Congratula-
tions."

Harry Truman was indeed going somewhere. His
Memoirs recall that "being a President is like riding a tiger."
What Truman rode was the swift current of irritated
public opinion flowing out of America's readjustment to
peacetime.

Less than three months after the Missouri Senator took
the oath as Vice-President, the death of Roosevelt cata-
pulted Truman into that elite circle of thirty-three men
who have held the office of Chief Executive of the
United States. During his years in office, the role of the

American President was to assume even greater power and prestige in the alliance of the free Western world against the Soviet bloc.

Throughout most of his nearly eight years in office, Truman was to have rough sledding with both the public and official Washington. Controversy still rages over the assets and liabilities of his administration. He is probably still too recent in history to be judged. But what interests us here — as also with Presidents Roosevelt and Eisenhower — is not so much what President Truman actually did or did not accomplish as what the American voters *thought* he did.

The man who became our thirty-third President on April 12, 1945, is one of the seven Vice-Presidents in history who were elevated to the Presidency upon the death of the Chief Executive. He is one of only three (along with Theodore Roosevelt and Calvin Coolidge) who then went on to win the White House on their own right for a second term in office.

At one point, President Truman was to enjoy a greater popularity with the American public than did either Roosevelt or Eisenhower. Yet Truman was more often a *minority* than a *majority* President in the public opinion polls. In well over half of the time he was President, Truman had less than half of the American electorate approving of his performance in office in Gallup Poll checks on his popularity.

He insisted, in the face of much persuasion to the contrary by some of his advisers, on seeking re-election in 1948, and won. Yet his average popularity during his second term in office, an elected term, was actually below that of his first term when he was serving out Roosevelt's mandate.

His identification with FDR is significant in understanding the public's reaction. So long as he was wearing the mantle of the late President, he fared pretty well with the voters. In many respects, the combination of voting blocs forged by FDR during his twelve years in office had a lot to do with bringing Truman his victory in 1948. When Truman tried to go it alone, however, his performance with the public was likely to suffer — it seemed that he was much more popular as a substitute Roosevelt than as a real-life Truman.

The word of Roosevelt's death came to the people late in the afternoon of an early spring day near the end of the war in Europe. The nation went into a weekend of mourning. "Closed Out of Reverence" signs were in evidence in store windows across the country. A reaction typical of many millions of Americans was that of a Detroit woman — "He'll be on the air tomorrow to say it was all a mistake."

To a greater degree than any previous Chief Executive, Roosevelt had created an image of himself in voters' minds — one he constantly nourished and polished through radio speeches heard by millions across the nation. An estimated 53 million American adults, for example (70 per cent of the civilian adult population), heard one radio address by him in March, 1942.

During the twelve years of his administration, millions of Americans came to the conclusion that there were direct personal advantages in putting their faith and trust in this one man. This kind of attitude has caused reverberations on the political scene which we are still feeling.

Despite the voter's regard for Roosevelt personally (a regard chiefly instrumental in Roosevelt's 1936 triumph in the face of unpopular New Deal measures), it still took some schooling for FDR to teach the electorate that one man was more important than a tradition when it came to the question of a third term. When the issue first arose, the public vetoed the idea in a 1936 Gallup Poll with 62 per cent opposed to a third term for FDR and only 28 per cent in favor. By the eve of convention time in 1940, however, a majority had come around to the point of view that they would vote for Roosevelt if and when he sought another term.

A key argument in FDR's bid for a third and a fourth term was the familiar adage, "Don't change horses in midstream." That we were actually just entering the stream in 1940 and well out of the middle in 1944 was, of course, not apparent at the time to the American voter. By the time of the 1944 election, with the war's end still not immediately in sight to the public, it seemed almost natural for Roosevelt to run again. As early as the first part of 1943, a substantial majority (six out of ten) believed the President would try again; nearly as many said that if he did they thought they would support him. At the time of FDR's fourth inauguration, voters across the country thought that he would again be the Democratic nominee in 1948. Considering the threat from Russia which was apparent in 1948, it is highly possible, had Roosevelt lived, that the argument about not changing horses might have worked again.

FDR's teaching the American voter the advantages of voting for the man was to prove a blessing for the Republicans when Eisenhower arrived on the scene some years later. The degree to which he sold the Democratic party was anything but a blessing for the GOP — they still have to contend with the numerical superiority of the Democrats in every national election.

While Roosevelt was still in office, William Lydgate, in *What America Thinks,* described some of the source of the President's popularity as seen in Gallup Polls:

> In the eyes of a majority of voters . . . Roosevelt showed one chief virtue during his first three terms which more than offset his faults. That virtue in the minds of people — the thing which sustained the President's popularity in periods when he was being violently attacked — was sympathy for the common man. In singling out that virtue, people were of course reacting on the basis of instinct, feeling, emotion. They never categorized this appraisal into neat and logical compartments, or paraded facts, figures and illustrations to explain what they had in mind when they spoke of Roosevelt the friend of man. They resorted to generalities which sounded vague, but which were deeply and sincerely meant.

This Roosevelt appeal to the "forgotten man" in the dark depression days of the early 1930s is an appeal that the Republicans are still forced to battle. It is the main reason why the GOP is the minority party in United States politics.

Until 1952, the Republicans were unable to find a candidate possessing enough of that same appeal to the common man to offset the New Deal-oriented Democratic strength. In that year, these two legacies of the Roosevelt era — the appeal of the Democratic party and the importance of voting for the man — met head on, greatly frustrating the American voter in the process. It was not until 1956 that the voter found a cure for his frustrations. The political picture may be years in getting back into focus because of the cure the voter hit upon.

At the time of Roosevelt's death, a study by the *New York Herald Tribune* among voters across the country showed 70 per cent approving of the way FDR was handling the conduct of the war. At no point during the ten years in which the Gallup Poll checked FDR's popularity did it find less than half of the voters approving of his general handling of the Presidency.

President Truman has recorded in his *Memoirs* some of his feelings as he took over the Presidency: "During those first few hours, painful as they were because of our tragic loss, my mind kept turning to the task I had inherited and to the grave responsibilities that confronted our nation at that critical moment in history."

One task that the new President inherited was that of substituting as fully as possible for the commanding personality of Roosevelt. Considering the relatively short period in which people had to judge, the overwhelming approval of Truman recorded by the Gallup Poll in its first popularity check was probably more a measure of what the public *hoped* Truman would do than a record of what they actually thought he had *done* during his first two months in office.

Approval of the new President was widespread throughout all major population groups. The resounding vote of confidence from 87 per cent (Roosevelt's high was 84 per cent, Eisenhower's thus far has been 79 per cent) was made up of endorsements both from liberal Democrats who looked for Truman to continue the policies of the late President and from conservative Republicans who believed he would be safer than FDR. Businessmen thought Truman would be friendlier than Roosevelt toward business; industrial workers saw in him another champion of labor.

As long as there was the exhilaration of winning the war, Truman fared well with the public. At a time, in July, 1945, when a majority of voters across the country wanted the Democrats to win the Presidency in 1948, the President was the choice of six out of ten Democratic voters to head their party's 1948 ticket. Trouble was brewing for the Democratic administration, however, and it would erupt in the form of strikes as the war came to a close.

In September, the first full month of peacetime in nearly four years, over 400,000 workers were on strike — twice the number on strike in August. By October, some 800,-000 workers were out. Labor stoppages of every variety spread into various industries. In a show of strength, the National Federation of Telephone Workers suspended transcontinental telephone service in every state from 2 to 6 P.M. on October 5. Because of a longshoremen's strike, the *Queen Elizabeth* in New York harbor had to be unloaded by military troops. In Hollywood, five hundred pickets walked their beats in front of the major film studios. By the first of 1946, nearly a million and a half men were out.

President Truman's popularity did not immediately feel the full effects of the public's discontent. In early November, he still had the approval of 82 per cent of the voters. Once started down, however, his popularity slipped fast. By the end of November it was down to 75 per cent. By February, 1946, it stood at 63 per cent — a disaffection on the part of one voter in four since the President had gone into office less than a year before. Truman's popularity hit the 50 per cent line in April; it would not rise above it again until some time after the November Congressional elections when the Republicans swept to a landslide victory (their first Congressional victory since 1930) and won control of the House of Representatives by a 58-seat margin.

What Truman was facing during these months was a public disillusioned with the evaporation of their postwar dream world. It is questionable whether any Chief Executive could have stemmed the tide of reconversion resentment. The economic upheaval was an inevitable by-product of reconversion; the political disaster for the Democrats was an even more inevitable by-product of that economic upheaval.

A quick rundown on the mood of the people during 1946

reveals no single overriding issue which caused the Democrats' fall from grace. It was more a collection of growing disenchantments with the world the Truman administration had inherited — a world of strikes and labor disputes, constantly rising prices and fights over price controls, and a wartime ally who refused to behave the way we had expected.

It seemed as if everybody had their gripes. When the Gallup Poll asked America's wives what their husbands' chief faults were, only four in a hundred could think of nothing about their spouse which irritated them. The number one fault of husbands, the wives said, was that they drank too much. The women also complained that their men were thoughtless and selfish.

When husbands were given a chance to retaliate, their chief complaint could be summed up in the reply one gave a Gallup Poll reporter — "Nag, nag, nag — she's *driving* me to drink!" Men also griped about their wives' extravagance and their poor homemaking.

With the strike problem near its peak in 1946, new labor legislation was seen as the primary issue of the coming Congressional campaign. The total number of strikes in 1946 did not greatly surpass the 1945 total. But what strikes there were involved more men (about a million more) and, above all, were longer — the total number of days men were idle because of labor stoppages in 1946 was three times as great as it had been in 1945.

President Truman's suggestion for a thirty-day cooling-off period before a major strike could be called met with widespread approval in all occupation groups (including the union rank and file). But this did not necessarily help his popularity — it was more a question of supporting *anything* advanced as a solution to the labor problem.

As Truman's popularity descended toward the 50 per cent line, the public's criticism of him, in fact, was centered on his handling of the strike situation. Along with this was the belief that the President was leaving the middle of the road (a route a majority consistently wanted

TRUMAN AND THE "MIDDLE ROAD"

	Wanting HST "In the Middle"	Believing HST "Moving Left"
October, 1945	55	10
February, 1946	52	44

Truman to follow) and moving to the left to side more with labor.

As the President appeared to head left, he and his party lost much of the faith that the electorate had had in their handling of labor disputes. The question, to the public, was becoming one of vested interests. By midsummer, the weight of sentiment among the American public opposed the President's handling of the strike situation.

WHO CAN HANDLE STRIKES BEST?

	Democrats	Republicans	No Difference
October, 1945	41	31	28
February, 1946	36	36	28
October, 1946	23	46	31

Even at their peak, of course, the strikes directly involved only a relatively small proportion of the total public. Indirectly, however, they affected a great many voters.

In terms of those more directly concerned — the rank and file of union labor — the Democrats' "mismanagement" (or what was thought to be that) of the strike problem meant a shift of about ten points to the Republicans — from the 72 per cent of union members who voted for Roosevelt in 1944 down to 62 per cent who favored the Democrats early in 1946. The GOP had made a sizable dent in this traditionally Democratic bloc.

The indirect effect of the labor unrest was also bad for the Democrats. The belief that the Democrats were catering to union labor showed up in the shift to the Republicans in two groups largely without labor organization — white-collar workers and farmers. The Democrats were losing them coming and going — union labor for not doing enough, non-union workers for doing too much.

In calling attention to the whole question of wages and prices, the strikes intensified the mounting concern with the rising cost of living. As the end of the summer signaled the kickoff of the regular 1946 campaign, inflation was named as the chief problem facing the country. More than nine out of ten voters expected prices to keep rising that autumn.

Evidence that rising prices were not something for just the man of the house to worry about appeared in another Gallup Poll at the time. More than three out of ten American homes reported that the wife alone handled the family's money matters. In another four out of ten homes, the husband and wife together worked out the budget, leaving only a minority of families where the man was sole controller of the household finances.

As the 1946 election approached, the cost of living index showed a 20 per cent rise over the previous twelve months. In one month alone this normally slow-moving barometer of costs jumped eight percentage points. The typical American non-farm family estimated they spent $17 a week on food. In 1942, the average had been $11.50 a week.

Perhaps the most surprising thing about the political scene in 1946 was that the Democrats managed to hold their lead in the race for Congress as late as they did. There was certainly enough dissatisfaction apparent early in the year to warrant a heartfelt desire to "throw the rascals out." The almost reluctant trend to the GOP in 1946 was evidence of how strong had been the Roosevelt administration's hold on certain blocs of voters.

It was not until July, in fact, that the Republicans pulled out ahead of the Democrats in Gallup Polls. From there on, however, there was no turning back until the voters had had their say about the postwar resentment they were feeling.

DEMOCRATIC DECLINE
— 1946 —
Congressional Preferences

	Democrat	Republican
February	55	45
March	53	47
July	49	51
October	47	53
November Election	45.7	54.3

Much more than being a victory for the Republicans, the 1946 elections were a defeat for President Truman. It was the first opportunity that voters had to express their growing dissatisfaction with the way they felt he was running the country.

After the voting, it seemed almost as if the electorate had gotten something off their chest and now could get back to normal. The Democratic outlook soon got brighter in almost every respect. The cost of living index held still, if only briefly. The typical American could see no depression ahead in 1947. In the early months of the year, optimism about the Russians cooperating with us in world affairs was more marked. The winter of our discontent with the Democrats was over.

In January, 1947, President Truman's popularity showed its first upturn in a year and a half. By March, six out of ten voters across the country approved of the way he was running the White House.

In some official circles, the President even appeared to be growing more friendly with the right wing. GOP Floor Leader Charles Halleck got off the crack: "Harry knows a trend when he sees one. Why, I expect any day now to see him register as a Republican." In point of fact, the President did appear to the voters to be veering to the right. But in so doing, he was only coming from the unpopular left and moving into that highly popular middle of the road. As Truman did so, his popularity continued on the upswing.

The Democrats' chances of taking the White House improved markedly. Trailing the Republicans badly in the aftermath of the 1946 elections, they moved out ahead of them in the spring of 1947. By May, a clear majority of voters (57 per cent) wanted the Democrats in 1948.

Democratic pessimism about their chances in 1948 began to evaporate (they now thought they had at least an even chance of winning) while GOP voters were far less sure of a victory — an event that had seemed almost a foregone conclusion in the ranks of both parties immediately following the November, 1946, election.

President Truman's popularity slipped a little during 1947 — 60 per cent approval in March to 52 per cent in November. But for Truman this was relatively calm — in most other years of his Administration his voter popularity was likely to fluctuate 20 to 30 points.

The trend to the Democrats that year was really nothing more than a return to the fold on the part of old-time Roosevelt supporters. The renewed strength of the Democrats came from such traditionally FDR voters as manual workers, big-city voters and younger voters — the voters who kept electing Roosevelt term after term. In addition, the Democrats now had the support of the nation's farmers — a traditionally Republican group (at least outside the South) who had gotten to like the high prices they were receiving under Democratic farm programs.

Two major concerns came to dominate the public's thinking in 1947 — the rising cost of living and the growing threat of Russia. Throughout the year, these two worries weave in and out of poll findings. The Democrats had the upper hand in dealing with both of these problems as far as most voters were concerned.

Two of our minor concerns in 1947 — neither with any particular political implications — were the Flying Saucer scare in the summer and the lowered hemlines of Christian Dior's "New Look" in the fall.

The saucers were first reported on June 25th. By early August, 90 per cent of Americans in a Gallup Poll said they had heard something about them. The public's theories as to what they were varied widely. About one person in three admitted he didn't know what they were. About the same number attributed them to overactive imaginations. Others thought they were a hoax, while about one American in eight held to the opinion that they were a secret weapon of our own. Only a negligible few feared it was something the Russians had cooked up; almost nobody thought the flying disks came from outer space (or if they did they wouldn't admit it to Gallup Poll reporters).

Dior's below-the-knee skirts arrived with the new Paris fashions in the early fall. They had, if anything, greater impact than flying saucers — by late September, Gallup Poll reporters encountered only about five Americans in every hundred who had not heard of the New Look. Both men and women initially said they didn't like the longer skirts. About four women in every ten, however, favored the new style — or more than enough to start the trend which ultimately brought a New Look wardrobe into millions of American closets.

How much impact all of this clothes buying had on the cost of living is hard to say. By the end of 1947 the cost of living index was up 15 per cent over what it had been

58

in January. As early as May, in fact, rising prices were the top concern of families across the country. The Democrats' advantage from this was seen on several public opinion barometers. The public wanted the Democrats in office in the event depression hard times came again. And the public thought the Democrats were the best party to keep wages high.

When people were asked which item on a list they were shown they would be most interested in knowing more about, they picked "The Relationship Between Wages and Prices" by a slim margin over "The Russian-American Conflict." Both were in the forefront on the public's mind in 1947.

The year's international news tells quickly why the public's earlier optimism about Russia's cooperating with us died fast. The score in the cold war in 1947 was tied — Russia got Hungary and Rumania, we held Greece and Turkey.

President Truman's offensive in the new struggle advocating immediate aid for Greece and Turkey met with wide public acceptance. The President's speech to Congress and the nation on March 12, 1947, made a favorable impression: Three fourths of all voters interviewed by the Gallup Poll afterwards said they had heard or read about the speech. There was some regret that the problem had not first been sent to the United Nations.

Above all, however, people seemed to realize that this was not just a temporary commitment — that once set on a policy of opposition to Russia, it would be hard to turn back. The prevailing public sentiment can be summed up in the statement of a Philadelphia woman, an office manager, who told a Gallup Poll reporter: "If we let Russia get away with her aggressive policy, she'll start reaching out for more and more and then we're bound to have a war on our hands. Dictators never know when to stop if you appease them. Putting our foot down like this is more likely to bring peace."

From a speech by the Secretary of State at Harvard's Commencement that June came the second of two cold war victories scored by the Truman administration in 1947 — the Marshall Plan. When General Marshall proposed that the United States "Do whatever it is able to do to assist in the return of normal economic health in the world," his words did not receive the immediate widespread public interest that Truman's speech on Greece and Turkey had. But among many of those who knew what was involved in the Marshall Plan (an ever-growing number of the public throughout the year), the idea was warmly endorsed. As the plan got wider circulation, the proportion of voters supporting it remained relatively constant.

When the concern over the high cost of living conflicted in voters' minds with worry over the threat of Russia, the latter generally emerged the winner. At a time when the American people admitted that they were having a rough time of it financially in making ends meet (and husbands and wives acknowledged that money problems were the chief cause of most of their arguments), the public still voted for aid to Europe to ward off Communist infiltration over a tax reduction. Stopping

Communism was more urgent than making ends meet.

At the beginning of 1948, therefore, the Democrats entered the Presidential race holding an advantage with the voters over the GOP in handling the two big problems facing the country. They held a comfortable majority over the Republicans in terms of which party (irrespective of candidates) the electorate wanted to see take the White House in the fall. Truman's popularity in January, 1948, had firmed up at about 52 or 53 per cent. A test run of the President's chances against Governor Thomas Dewey found Truman in the lead running a slightly stronger race against the New York Governor, in fact, than he had the previous summer.

The scene had not yet been completely taken over by the coming political fight. Dr. Kinsey's famous report — published in December, 1947 — stirred up a great deal of controversy. A Gallup Poll on the subject found that 57 per cent of the public thought the book reporting sexual behavior of the American male was a good thing. Only 11 per cent objected to the report.

Political interest mounted as the season of state primaries opened. And in a few short months, the political picture was completely changed. The Democrats appeared to be reeling in confused fashion towards an almost certain defeat in November. President Truman, trailing Dewey in a Gallup Poll test of the two men's chances, was being pressured from certain quarters not to seek re-election. Some of the atmosphere of gloom in the Democratic camp is suggested by Raymond Moley's description of the situation in the March 8, 1948, issue of *Newsweek*:

61

On the 15th anniversary of its rise to power, the Democratic party is returning to the primeval chaos from which FDR lifted it. Minorities are not only drifting away; they are splitting up. Minority groupism as a political faith is at the end of its sandy rope . . .

Truman simply does not have what it takes to bring masses of city voters enthusiastically, almost fanatically, to vote Democratic. The vast majorities in the big Northern cities were not voting Democratic in the past 15 years. They were voting Roosevelt.

In certain respects, Moley was right — Truman did not have what it takes to carry the traditional Roosevelt blocs by himself. But the Democratic party did. On Election Day in November, the big city voters and other traditional Democratic blocs were still "voting Roosevelt."

In essence, the 1948 election was pretty much a straight party-line affair in which the numerically superior Democrats outvoted the Republicans. As an added help, they had the majority support of the Independent voters. No matter what their past voting record, the description "Independent" fits, if only as a convenient way of labeling those voters who refuse of their own accord to classify themselves officially as Republicans or Democrats. Actually, the Independents had been heavily Democratic in their voting preferences throughout most of the Roosevelt era. In 1946 the Independents turned sour on the Democrats and a majority who voted cast a Republican ballot. In 1948 they were back in the Democratic column where they were to stay until the personality of Eisenhower attracted a substantial majority in 1952.

The 1948 election can also be called a victory for Roosevelt — convincing evidence of the "almost fanatically" loyal support built up by FDR. When millions of voters came to the conclusion that neither Truman nor Dewey had the qualities of leadership they were looking for, they either stayed away from the voting booth (the 1948 turnout was lower than in any other Presidential election in twenty years) or returned to voting habits built up during 1932 through 1944.

Throughout the 1948 campaign, the Democratic party had an edge in basic party strength. When Dewey reached probably the peak of his popular strength (right after the nominating conventions), voters still picked the Democratic party as the one they wanted to win the White House if candidates were no consideration. The Democrats also had an edge in terms of which party the voters believed to be best able to handle the problems that they, the voters themselves, considered important.

1948 ELECTION
— Party Strength —

Voters Calling Themselves	Per Cent	Estimated No.
Democrats	45	22,000,000
Republicans	35	17,000,000
Independents	19	9,500,000
Other party	1	500,000

— Actual Voting —

	Per Cent	Votes Cast
Truman	49.9	24,179,623
Dewey	45.3	21,991,290
States' Rights	2.4	1,176,154
Progressive	2.4	1,157,326

63

In winning the election, President Truman trailed behind his party. He received 49.9 per cent of the popular vote; Democratic candidates for Congress that year polled 53.7 per cent, or about what Roosevelt had received in 1944.

As the table shows, only about one voter in a hundred in the 1948 electorate actually considered himself a member of an official party other than Republican or Democratic. Yet on Election Day, nearly 5 per cent of the voters cast their ballot for either the States' Rights or Progressive ticket. At one point in the campaign, these splinter groups had the support of some 12 per cent of the electorate. The biggest trouble the Democrats had in 1948 came not so much from the GOP as it did from the extreme left and right wings of the Democratic party itself. The Dixiecrats on the right and the Progressives on the left nearly pulled the Democratic party apart.

The Democratic high command had gathered in Washington in mid-February, 1948, for the traditional Jefferson-Jackson Day dinner. Events of that week gave ample reason for their general aura of gloom. On Tuesday, in a Congressional by-election in New York's Bronx, the American Labor Party candidate Leo Isacson, backed by Henry Wallace, won an amazing 2 to 1 victory over the candidate of Ed Flynn's Democratic machine — amazing since registered Democrats outnumbered registered ALP voters by more than 3 to 1 in this supposedly safe Democratic district.

The following day Wallace announced that he had 464,000 signatures from California and needed only 189,-

000 more to get on the ballot for that state's twenty-five electoral votes. On Friday, fifty-two Southern Congressmen adopted a resolution condemning Truman's civil rights program. On Saturday, the Americans for Democratic Action met for a three-day convention in Philadelphia and promptly put on the record a sharp criticism of the President and refused to endorse his candidacy at that time. As dissatisfaction such as this grew within the Democratic party, Truman's stock with voters fell fast during the spring and early summer.

Henry Wallace's initial strength (he announced his candidacy in January) was frightening to the Democrats. His support centered in the states of the Middle Atlantic and East Central area where nearly two hundred electoral votes were at stake. Even with Roosevelt, the Democrats had normally only just about broken even in the popular vote in these two regions.

In the big cities, Wallace was polling about 15 per cent of the vote in the spring — enough to make the poll vote for Truman and Dewey uncomfortably close for the Democrats. In Chicago, Wallace's 12 per cent in a poll left Truman with 42 per cent, Dewey with 41 per cent. In California, with Truman and Dewey dead even at 42 per cent, Wallace had 10 per cent. His 7 per cent in Pennsylvania, had it been in its normally Democratic column, would have given the lead in that state to Truman. Without it, the President trailed Dewey.

Although generally from the left, Wallace's backers could not be described as particularly united behind a single cause — a Gallup Poll report described them as a "conglomeration of protesters." What they were chiefly protesting against was Harry S. Truman.

Actually, the Wallace supporters interviewed by the Gallup Poll disagreed with their Presidential candidate on many issues, particularly regarding our policy toward Russia. Wallace opposed the European Recovery Plan, they favored it. They thought Russia was aggressive and out to dominate the world; Wallace based his program on other assumptions. Wallace was against increased defense spending; his supporters questioned by the Gallup Poll favored more military spending. One place where Wallace and his "conglomeration" were in accord was in their attitude toward Truman — they were agin' him.

There were undoubtedly Communist sympathizers in the Progressive cause. On May Day in New York City, two thousand persons from the Communist wing of the Progressive Party paraded in protest against the showing of *The Iron Curtain,* a movie about the Gouzenko spy case in Canada. In the riots that followed, the protesters battled ex-GIs from veterans organizations all the way from Madison Square Garden to Times Square. Events such as these undoubtedly had much to do with the belief of a majority of Americans in a Gallup Poll that summer that the Progressive Party was dominated by Communists.

The day before the New York May Day riots, the second of the two splinter groups which plagued the Democrats in 1948 was meeting in Jackson, Mississippi. Bringing to a climax the chain of events set in motion by Truman's proposed Fair Employment Practices Commission, the Dixiecrats officially proclaimed themselves revolters from the Democratic party. Of the ten Southern states represented at the Dixiecrat convention, only four would ultimately wind up in the States' Rights column in November.

The public surveyed had voted its support of the President's FEPC program when Truman first proposed it in the fall of 1947. Southern voters, however, were flatly opposed to the plan (one criticism offered by voters both North and South was that it wouldn't work because so many people were opposed to it).

From its beginnings in February with the Southern Manifesto in Congress, the Dixiecrat revolt quickly swept the Southern grass roots, spurred by the white Southerners' dislike of the civil rights program. In South Carolina, one county's convention delegates heard their county chief read a resolution by which the county "seceded" from the Democratic party. As the delegates roared their ayes to the resolution, a banner was raised in the back of the hall. On it was printed a parody of a popular song of the time: "You can have her, we don't want her, she's too black for me."

In understanding something of the popular sentiment in the Dixiecrat revolt, the close tie-in between States' Rights strength and intensity of feeling about the Negro question should be kept in mind. The rights of individual states may have been the surface issue; below the surface was the boiling turbulence of the racial issue. As V. O. Key points out in *Southern Politics*:

> The most intense support for the 1948 southern revolt came from the areas with most Negroes. The foundations of the revolt were symbolized in its presidential and vice-

67

presidential candidates, J. Strom Thurmond of South Carolina and Field Wright of Mississippi, chief executives of the two states with the highest proportion of Negro population.

That this revolt should be sparked by a civil rights program sponsored by Truman — a former border-state Senator with a generally safe record on this issue as far as the South was concerned — serves to confirm the fact that the Dixiecrats, like the Wallace supporters, were protesting much more about the policies of President Truman than about the policies of the Democratic party. While the Dixiecrat revolt was spreading, Truman's popularity in the South dropped 24 points — in October, 1947, six out of ten Southerners had given the President a vote of confidence; by April, 1948, nearly the same percentage of Southerners were dissatisfied with Truman's performance in office.

The President's national popularity felt the effects of this struggle within the Democratic party. Truman's popularity across the country dropped from 53 per cent in January to 36 per cent approval in April. He lost heavily among voters who had supported Roosevelt in 1944. In January, the President had a vote of confidence from two out of three persons who had voted for FDR in 1944; by April his popularity with these voters had dropped to 45 per cent.

In all the pulling and tugging, voters came to reason that if Truman wasn't able to hold his own party together, he was hardly the kind of national leader they wanted. He was criticized by the public for being inconsistent, for being too easily swayed, for not standing firm under fire.

Just what kind of man *were* the American people looking for in 1948? A Gallup Poll at the time asked people what they would do if they were President; the answers are revealing as to the type of leader we had in mind as being ideal.

We wanted a President, above all else, to be a humanitarian, a benevolent helper, and a protector of the common man. Here are some descriptions taken at random: "I would try to do something to make the people in the slums happier." "So many children don't get enough to eat, I'd want to try to help." "I'd fight for the poor people and see that they don't get fooled by the rich and greedy."

By flanking these descriptions with others recorded of Roosevelt during his lifetime, the answer is clear as to just whom the voters would have *liked* to have voted for in 1948 had there been an opportunity: "He champions the poor." "He gave the forgotten man a break." "He took the government away from the rich and gave it back to the people." "He fights to protect the weak."

Neither Truman nor Dewey seemed to have enough of these desired qualities. Early in 1948, a survey asked voters what they would say to a friend if they were talking about some of the leading Presidential candidates. In Truman's case, derogatory phrases outweighed words of praise by a ratio of about 5 to 3, with "inefficient," "incapable," "weak," and "no ideas of his own" the kind of comments mentioned frequently. With Dewey, favorable comments outnumbered unfavorable ones by about 3 to 2. But about one voter in four said he just didn't know enough about the New York Governor to say anything about him. Only one in fourteen said this about Truman.

The President thus had many apparent weaknesses to voters. Dewey had a better image among those who knew him — but he was an unknown quality to a substantial number. For a period both before and after the nominating conventions, the public apparently felt that the unknown potential was a better choice than the known weakness. This is probably one of the major reasons why Dewey kept slightly ahead of Truman in popular strength through the early stages of the fall campaign.

As voting time neared, several new developments served to help the Truman cause. On October 18 farm prices dropped sharply and many normally Republican farmers in the Midwest decided that their economic future would be more secure with the Democratic farm program. A Californian felt he would lose his vote if he gave it to Wallace — and gave it instead to Truman. A New York housewife wavering between Dewey and Truman heard one of the President's fiery speeches late in the campaign and decided Truman was her man. This suggests a few of the specific reasons why so many voters swung to Truman during the last month.

In a general sense, however, many millions of voters came to feel that the gamble on the unknown quality in Dewey was too risky. If Truman seemed to have his weaknesses, he also had one strong point — he was a member of the party of Roosevelt. When the chips were down, these millions of voters decided their safest bet was a vote for Roosevelt, or the best substitute they could find — the Democratic party. It was President Truman's good fortune to be the Democratic candidate.

A Gallup Poll taken shortly after the 1948 election indicated that some 13 million adults (about one in seven) frequently had trouble getting to sleep at night. Certainly included among them in the nights after Truman's victory were many of the pollsters themselves.

The comedians had a field day with the public opinion polls after their forecast that Governor Dewey would win. Fred Allen said, "This year the polls went to the dogs, instead of the other way around." Another radio comedian commented, "Truman is the first President to lose in a Gallup and win in a walk," while still another punned, "the public opinion pollsters committed Deweycide." The Chicago *Daily News*, reporting the general disillusionment with the polls, told of an elderly woman bus rider who put down her newspaper, turned to her companion and said: "Now I don't know whether to believe even the Kinsey Report."

Why did the polls go wrong in their final forecast?

The chief error lay in the fact that practically all of the public opinion polls stopped their interviewing too early in the campaign. With the Gallup Poll, interviewing in the final survey was completed on October 15, eighteen days before Election Day. The survey did not catch the last-minute trend to the Democrats among such groups as Midwestern farmers, disillusioned Wallace supporters, and wavering voters who made up their mind after hearing one of Truman's "give-'em-hell" speeches in the closing

71

days of the campaign. A post-election analysis showed that a minimum of 4.5 million Truman votes (nearly one out of five in his total vote) was based on decisions by voters *after* the middle of October.

In its final election report, for example, the Gallup Poll showed the Progressive Party ticket with 4 per cent of the vote. As the voting neared, many Wallace supporters deserted him to return to their normal Democratic ballot. Wallace actually polled 2.4 per cent of the vote.

There was an unusually high proportion of voters in the final October 15 survey who were undecided between Truman and Dewey. Fourteen per cent of all persons fell into the undecided category — more than enough to give the victory to either candidate. On the basis of past experience, it was assumed that this group would probably vote in such small numbers that they could be eliminated from consideration. As it turned out, many of them did vote and they voted about 3 to 1 for Truman.

Finally, the problem of voting turnout was particularly acute in 1948. In any election survey, there is a certain percentage of persons who say they are planning to vote and then, for one reason or another, do not get to the polling place. Their candidate preferences must, in effect, be deducted from the final results of the poll. The total number voting in 1948 was about one half of the potential voting population at that time. With the public opinion polls sampling the total potential voting population, the difficulty was in ascertaining *which* half of the potential electorate would vote, which would not.

Since the 1948 election, the Gallup Poll has tried to take

into account the sources of error that year. Interviewing now continues until the Saturday before election — about sixty hours before the polls open on Election Day. Interviewers telegraph their final reports to the Gallup Poll headquarters where last-minute shifts in opinion can be plotted against earlier ascertained data. Undecided voters are now questioned intensively to determine how they are likely to vote. And all voters are asked a battery of questions especially designed to determine whether or not they will actually get to the polling booth. From the errors made in 1948 came many valuable improvements in public opinion polling methods.

During his second term in office, President Truman's popularity with voters hit its lowest point in the late winter of 1951. The Communists in Korea had just broken off the truce talks once again and it seemed to the public as if the police action there might drag on forever. Behind the public's bitterness about Korea were attitudes which had been taking shape for a number of years regarding Russia and international Communism. Just how these attitudes took form, and what caused them, were determined in various public opinion poll findings from the mid-1930s until the eve of the outbreak of war in Korea.

4

The Shotgun Marriage Breaks Up

From Yalta to the Yalu

As a sidelight on the Washington scene at Christmas 1944, a national newsmagazine reported the case of a Washington carpenter who had received an unexpected Yuletime gift of four bottles of imported liquor and four boxes of candy. The package, delivered by a chauffeur in a black sedan, had enclosed a crested engraved card which read: "The Government Purchasing Commissar of the Soviet Union in the U.S.A. extends season's greetings." The name of the very much surprised carpenter was Harry Dexter White.

The episode is offered not as a comment on the dark implications of the *other* Harry Dexter White, of the Treasury Department, being on the Soviets' gift list. After a decade and a half of the cold war, the story's chief interest is in the light manner in which it was reported — very much in the same vein as those human interest notes which radio and TV commentators like to offer as they sign off the air. It stands as a good comment on the general American attitude toward the Russians in those closing days of World War II.

After Korea, Hungary, Tibet and numerous other instances of Communist aggression over the past fifteen years, it may seem inconceivable to some that we, the American people, were ever really friendly toward the Russians.

Yet in early 1945, the public clearly welcomed the Russians as allies and counted on their friendship in the postwar world. A majority of the American people in a Gallup Poll in February, 1945, said they believed the Soviet Union could be trusted to cooperate with us in world affairs after the war. Seven out of ten Americans favored the idea of sending German men to Russia to help rebuild her war-shattered cities. Only a negligible minority of 6 per cent of the public was disappointed in the results of the Yalta Conference.

Less than one year later, the picture had sharply changed. The Russian army had seized American-owned oil refineries in Hungary. The Gouzenko spy case in Canada, with all its frightening implications, was beginning to break into the public press. The first meeting of the United Nations General Assembly was hopelessly bogged down over the Russians' refusal to pull their troops out of revolt-torn Iran. Faced with developments like this, a majority of the American public had come to view the chances of Soviet cooperation with us in a pessimistic light. By the middle of 1946, nearly six out of ten Americans diagnosed Russia's intentions as those of a nation building up to be *the* ruling power in the world.

75

In that one year, much of the public's hope for a peaceful world had been shattered. Our confidence in Russia, built up slowly over the war years, had waned with each new Soviet threat or aggression.

There are certainly few instances in the nation's history where public opinion has been literally *forced* to make such a complete about-face. The Japanese attack on Pearl Harbor had surprised Americans in its timing perhaps, but it followed a fairly long period in which we had come to the conclusion that Japan's basic aims were a danger to democracy. We had some six or seven years to come to the decision that Hitler was America's enemy — and that decision had its foundation in an earlier conflict in which Americans fought Germans. The decision on Russia had to be reached in a matter of months.

The unmasking of Russia did not come as a total surprise to the American public. Long before the Second World War and, in fact, all through our wartime alliance with Russia, a substantial number of Americans were suspicious of Soviet intentions. In earlier years, however, it was probably as much a suspicion of the unknown as it was a fear of the specific threat of international Communism. It seems a fairly safe bet that few Americans between the two world wars paid much attention to the whole question.

There are no polling results from the 1920s to indicate specifically how Americans lined up on the issue of Communism. One hardly needs a public opinion poll, however, to surmise that the marriage of Douglas Fairbanks and Mary Pickford had far greater public interest than did the news of the Harding administration's decision to with-hold diplomatic recognition of the new Bolshevik government.

The size of the Communist party vote in this country during the 1920s and 1930s certainly indicated that this particular philosophy had little appeal to the electorate.

COMMUNIST PARTY VOTING STRENGTH

Year	Communist Vote	Total Vote
*1924	36,386	29,090,926
*1928	48,770	36,772,922
1932	102,991	39,747,349
1936	80,159	45,647,117
1940	46,251	49,815,312

*William Z. Foster on Workers ticket

If the total number voting Communist at the 1932 high point were tripled (on the assumption that some sympathizers might not feel strongly enough actually to vote for the party), the number would still make up less than one per cent of the electorate.

When public opinion poll findings became regularly available in the mid-1930s, the issue of Communism and its potential menace had already been considerably clouded by the increasing threat of Nazism. By 1936, the world had seen in Germany the Reichstag fire, the outlawing of all but the Nazi party, and the legal persecution of the Jews. In March of 1936, German troops reoccupied the Rhineland.

Early poll findings do indicate that the American public was not favorably disposed toward Communism. A

1937 Gallup Poll recorded a majority in favor of a law permitting a ban on any printing firm producing Communist literature. But successive moves by Hitler brought Americans to the realization that for the moment at least, Nazism was a greater danger than Communism. When asked in 1938 whether they would prefer to see the Russians or the Germans emerge as victor in the event of a war between the two totalitarians, 85 per cent of those with opinions favored a Russian victory. About three persons in ten had no opinion.

The public's attitude toward the Spanish Civil War shows some of this same pattern of siding, if only vaguely, with any cause which appeared to be opposing fascism.

Perhaps the most surprising thing about the Spanish Civil War is that so few in the public actually came to the point of taking sides in any way. In the winter of 1937, when the first American contingents in the International Brigade were going into action around Madrid, two out of three people back home said they had either not followed the events in Spain or had no real preference between Franco's rebels and the government forces. In 1937, millions of Americans still hoped that the European conflict would leave the United States untouched. Among those Americans who did have an opinion, however, sentiment heavily favored the Loyalists. Clearly involved in the disapproval of Franco was his identification with Hitler and Mussolini.

Although pro-Loyalist sentiment made up only a small segment of public opinion, attitudes such as these, favorable toward any anti-Nazi, helped to foster the general public acceptance of the Russians as allies in World War II.

Russia herself did little to help her cause in America when she invaded Finland and Poland in 1939. The Finnish cause particularly — with its white-clad ski troopers and that country's fully paid-up war debt — stirred great public sympathy in this country. By 1941, after the Nazis invaded Russia, sentiment was on the side of a Russian victory over Germany, but it had dropped off sharply since 1938.

Our entry into the European conflict in 1941 found American public opinion ready to tolerate Russia as an enemy of Nazism, but by no means of a mind to sanction her actions in other respects. What began was at best an uneasy alliance.

Three public opinion agencies — the Office of Public Opinion Research, the National Opinion Research Center and the Gallup Poll — which kept a check on the public's attitude toward Russia during the Second World War centered their efforts on one key question — could Russia be trusted to cooperate with us after the war?

Generally speaking, the public's confidence in Russia's postwar cooperation could be measured by the miles that the Red Army advanced against the Nazis. So long as Russia stayed strictly to military objectives and went about the business of winning the war, American faith in Soviet intentions held on. Whenever the Soviet Union seemed to be straying from this path and meddling in the internal affairs of another country — as, for example, in Greece late in 1943 — our confidence usually dropped sharply.

WILL RUSSIA COOPERATE AFTER THE WAR?
1942-1945

1942	Yes	No	Uncertain
February	38	37	25
June	41	33	26
November	52	26	22
1943			
January	46	29	25
June	48	27	25
December	51	27	22
1944			
January	40	37	23
June	47	36	17
November	47	35	18
1945			
February	55	31	14
May	45	38	17
August	54	30	16
October	41	43	16

No matter what we thought of Russia's postwar designs, however, we did seem to take a liking to the Russian people. It could not exactly be called an affection of one equal for another; it was more a case of condescending admiration for an inferior who was putting up an unexpectedly magnificent fight. Our admiration was created by reports such as the following about the defense of Stalingrad (in the *New York Times* in September, 1942):

Only stone houses remain in Stalingrad. The German pattern of bombing has reduced many of these to ruins. Although only a few buildings are fit to live in, they still provide cover in the violent fighting . . . Stalingrad is becoming converted into a honeycomb of defense for battles for every house and every street. Each house must become a fortress and each group of Red Army men a garrison.

When the public was asked in late 1942 to describe the Russian people from a list of adjectives, the two selected most frequently were "hard-working" and "brave." At the same time, in another poll, less than one American in

WHAT WE THOUGHT OF OUR ALLIES AND ENEMIES*
— 1942 —

Russians		Germans	
Hard-working	61%	Warlike	67%
Brave	48	Hard-working	62
Ordinary	25	Cruel	57
Radical	25	Treacherous	42
Progressive	24	Intelligent	41
Ignorant	20	Conceited	32
Honest	19	Progressive	32
Practical	18	Arrogant	31
Intelligent	16	Brave	30
Warlike	14	Quick-Tempered	25
British		Japanese	
Courageous	60%	Treacherous	73%
Conservative	54	Sly	63
Artistic	52	Cruel	56
Snobbish	50	Warlike	46
Loyal	48	Hard-working	39
Sportsmanlike	42	Conceited	27
Stubborn	40	Intelligent	25
Industrious	39	Brave	24
Selfish	32	Quick-tempered	21
Honest	32	Arrogant	21

*Ten most popular adjectives for each nationality from list of twenty-three. Study by Office of Public Opinion Research.

four conceded that the Russian people were a match for the American people in all important respects; more held the view that the Soviet people were not quite as good as Americans in most major aspects.

Neither our admiration of the Russian people nor our hope in postwar cooperation made Americans lose sight of the fact that the Soviet Union needed to be carefully watched when peace arrived. About one person in four, early in the war, was willing to let Germany remain a fairly strong country to offset Russia's postwar power. Two out of three persons believed that if Russia attempted to spread Communism in Europe following the war, we should do everything we could to keep her from succeeding. And four out of ten Americans (in a *Fortune* poll) feared that Russia would try to do just that — a fear that soon proved well warranted.

The high-water mark in the public's confidence in Russia came in February, 1945. It occurred, paradoxically, at a time when Soviet actions in liberating Poland were hardly calculated to produce confidence. Perhaps the explanation lies in the fact that with peace so tantalizingly close, it seemed to make sense to hope for Russian cooperation. A healthy measure of wishful thinking cleared up the whole perplexing problem of international relations so well. Such hope coincided with the high point in our confidence in the United Nations, and preceded by only a few months the high initial approval of President Truman. In each instance, it was probably a case of our *wishing* things to work out well.

By the end of 1945, our confidence in Russia had been

severely shaken. By the end of 1946, it lay completely shattered. Our faith in Russian cooperation took a sharp nose dive during the spring of 1945 as their delegate's shenanigans at the San Francisco conference, plus Russian arrogance in Poland, shook the public's confidence. The public's optimism reappeared briefly in the late summer after Russia's declaration of war on Japan — a step which we had come to doubt Russia would take. It is one of the ironies of the cold war that this last real upsurge in American faith in the Soviet Union was motivated by a move which ultimately led to the Korean war. Nine minutes after she declared war on Japan, Russia's troops, massed on the Manchurian and Korean borders, moved into these territories. When the Red Army finally quit Korea, it left behind a cadre of Communist troops who were well enough trained to give American GIs a bitter surprise when they first encountered them in the summer of 1950.

As the failure of the Foreign Ministers' conference in London and the hassle over atomic bomb secrets brought home the fact that many of the public's earlier fears about Russia were to be realized, the course of our confidence in Russia ran generally downhill.

The general tenor of U.S. public opinion in the years of the cold war was set in those disappointing months in 1945 and 1946. The first UN General Assembly met in London and was immediately preoccupied with the Russian involvement in Iran and the Soviet charges of British interference in Greece. Viewing the results of these proceedings, two out of three Americans in a poll said that Russia would be the most to blame if the UN failed.

Three out of four Americans disapproved generally of Russia's policies in foreign affairs. The shotgun marriage between Russia and the U.S. at the beginning of World War II was now in the divorce courts.

Some idea of the speed with which unfavorable opinion about Russia crystallized is shown in surveys which asked the public just what they thought we should do about the Soviet Union. In February, 1946, only four per cent were ready to go to war with Russia right then and there to stop her aggressions. By June of 1946 — less than a year after the end of the war — one person in four was willing to take this step.

In the months, and then years, of growing tension that followed, American public opinion hardened to a point where the very use of the words "Russia" or "Communism"

GROWING MISTRUST OF RUSSIA

Percentage Believing Russia "Out to Rule the World"

June, 1946	58
October, 1947	76
March, 1948	77
May, 1949	66
January, 1950	70

had to be carefully watched by polltakers lest they unwittingly load a question. As one nation after another fell into the Soviet orbit, the American people became prepared for the inevitable shock. The timing of the actual blow in Korea may have come as a surprise, but by 1950, no Communist-inspired aggression anywhere in the world was much of a surprise to the U.S. public.

The minority in 1945 who had feared the outbreak of war in twenty-five years grew by 1948 to a majority of more than three out of four. The fall of Czechoslovakia

FEAR OF WAR

Percentage Seeing United States in War Within Twenty-five Years

March, 1945	38
March, 1946	69
April, 1947	73
February, 1948	76

in February, 1948, only reinforced Americans' conviction that when that war did come, our enemy would be Russia.

In his book *How Nations See Each Other*, Hadley Cantril points out that the American people in 1948 were far more inclined to think of the Russian people in unfriendly terms than they were to think this way of either the Germans or the Japanese. Those same Russian people whom we had thought of as hard-working and brave back in 1942 were still regarded by Americans as hard workers. But in 1948 we picked a new adjective to replace "brave" — it was "cruel."

A favorite Soviet tactic throughout the cold war has been to try to make it appear that the opposition to Russian policies in the United States has been confined largely to Wall Street and the wealthy capitalist. In point of fact, the working population of this country — the factory hand, the farmer and the white-collar clerk — has been every bit as critical of Russia as the well-to-do person — and sometimes even more critical.

By 1948, no sharp cleavage in American opinion along social or economic lines stood out where Russia was concerned. Before reaching this unanimity, however, public opinion went through the ironic stage where the wealthier, better-educated groups in this country were more friendly toward Russia than were the manual workers, office clerks and others who make up the proletariat in Soviet propaganda bulletins.

In early 1946, for example, a clear majority of persons with only grade-school education distrusted Russia's intentions in world affairs. In the same survey, persons with college training were just as clearly optimistic about Russian cooperation with the United States.

In 1947, when voters in all walks of life were asked for their views on United States policy toward Russia, a majority in all occupation groups believed it was not tough enough. Manual workers were somewhat more inclined to this point of view, however, than were business and professional groups.

In short, Russian efforts to divide the people of the United States along class lines were simply not succeeding. In all groups, by the eve of the Korean war, there was a clear awareness of the Soviet threat and a determination to move to meet this threat if necessary.

It was not a case of warmongering (a description favored by Andrei Vishinsky in 1947 when talking about the U.S. State Department). There was a widespread American desire for peace throughout the early years of the cold war; it has not diminished in any sense since then. The public has been steadily in favor of trying to work out an agreement with Russia to ease cold war tensions. The American people have consistently taken the point of view that "it's always better to talk things over," approving of a meeting between the leaders of East and West at any point when such a question has been put to them by the polls.

Talking, however, did not mean appeasement. The public had a deep-seated fear of the consequences of this path. Many Americans felt that the Anglo-French appeasement of Hitler in the 1930s had much to do with eventual United States involvement in World War II. In the public's view, the best way to keep the peace is to make it clear to Russia that we are armed and ready to go to war if Russia should choose to provoke one.

Behind the public's determined opposition to Russia was a collection of impressions about just what it was that the Communists were trying to do. Whether real or fancied, these grievances help to explain some of the *why* of our fear of the Soviet Union.

One of our chief grievances was a belief that Communist Russia had embarked on a policy of systematically destroying the Christian religion wherever she could. In this regard, the cold war has had some of the aspects of a holy war. Religion is a serious business in America — over half of all Americans are in church on a typical Sunday. An overwhelming 95 per cent of the people say they believe in a Deity of some nature. Our favorite motto, we told Gallup Poll reporters, is the Golden Rule of "Do unto others as you would have others do unto you." In the face of facts such as these, the finding that three out of four Americans in 1947 believed that the Communists would destroy the Christian religion if they could emphasizes one of the more deep-seated fears of Russia.

As another grievance, we viewed Russia's refusal, in those days, to allow travelers and visitors behind the Iron Curtain as an unfriendly act. We are a nation that likes to hop in the car and go visit. Sunday afternoon pleasure riding was the favorite pastime in 1947 of more than half of all American families. Eight out of ten Americans say that their next-door neighbors are pleasant. Russia's drawing a tight veil of secrecy around her activities indicated unneighborliness to us. It signified that Russia was hiding something and possibly preparing for war against us.

Still another item in the bill of grievances we wanted to present to Russia was the question of the satellite nations. In 1947, Americans could name five nations — Poland, Yugoslavia, Czechoslovakia, Hungary and Albania — which they felt qualified as Soviet satellites. In all of these, Americans believed, Russia had gained control by conquest, intimidation, infiltration or by setting up a puppet government.

Finally, we blamed Russia overwhelmingly for having weakened and hurt the United Nations — an organization in which we placed great trust and hope. If our faith in the UN suffered at times, it was more often than not because of another Russian veto or a walk-out by her delegates.

The month of June, a Gallup Poll has discovered, is Americans' favorite month of the year. It is unlikely, however, that June of 1950 would win many popularity contests. The outbreak of war in Korea late that month meant the beginning of a long period during which the American public's confidence in our ability to defeat the Communists in a hot war was severely shaken.

In many ways, the sense of frustration and bitterness that set in shortly after the first reverses in Korea can be linked to the fact that Americans had gotten themselves psychologically ready to fight the Russians — with Europe the most likely battlefield for this conflict. Cantril, for example, shows how the public was "definitely Europe-oriented in its outlook on the world" in 1948 — a statement suggested by our tendency to select European peoples as those toward whom we felt either *most* or *least* friendly. Yet when the clash with Communism came, it occurred not in Europe against the Russians, but in a little-known Asian country against the North Koreans and their Chinese allies. We had been building up a resentment of the Red Army soldier; we had to take out this resentment on his Far Eastern substitute. When his stand-in instead started to take it out on us in the bitter winter fighting in northern Korea, it made it all the more humiliating.

President Truman's decision to send United States troops to the defense of South Korea met initially with widespread approval. Eight out of ten Americans in the early weeks of the war said they thought Truman had made the right move. The historic step proved to be a shot in the arm to the President's slumping personal popularity with voters. Gallup Polls had shown his popularity generally trending downward since the start of his second term in 1949. In the aftermath of his action on Korea, Truman's popularity took its first substantial upturn since his inauguration — from 37 per cent approving his performance in office before the North Korean invasion to 46 per cent approving just after the United States troops entered the fight.

The feeling of actually doing something about the Communist threat, of finally, after several years of seeing one country after another lost to the rival camp, taking a stand, contributed to the support of Truman's action in the early days of the Korean war.

Disillusionment soon set in, however. The sharp reverses suffered by American troops, the casualty lists from the Pusan perimeter, and, above all, the entrance of the Chinese Communists into the war, caused quick revision in Americans' thinking about the wisdom of our action in Korea. The chain of disasters brought the public quickly to the opinion that they had somehow been deceived by the administration. Adding to our bitterness was the belief that Washington had not taken the public's advice about keeping United States defenses strong.

Most Americans, before the entrance of the Chinese Communists, believed that the United States had a good if not excellent chance of defeating the Chinese army in a war. At the same time, the public had had for many months serious doubts about the defense preparations being made by the administration. When the retreat from the Yalu began in 1950, the typical American's reaction was probably either one of a stunned "Why didn't we know about this?" or a smug "I told you so."

The President's popularity quickly felt the impact of these events. By January, 1951, it had dropped ten points

WAS KOREA A WISE MOVE?
Percentage Believing It Was

1950	
July	81
August	65
1951	
January	38
March	39

from the early days of the war. Just how closely Americans tied their feelings about Truman to their disappointment over the course of the war shows up in an analysis of the President's popularity in March, 1951. Among those voters who felt the American entrance in the Korean

TRUMAN'S POPULARITY AND KOREAN WAR
— *March, 1951*—

View of Truman's Job:	Feel War Was Mistake	Feel War Was Not Mistake
Approve	17	37
Disapprove	70	46
No opinion	13	17

fighting was a mistake, seven out of ten disapproved of the way Truman was handling his job. Those who approved of our action in Korea gave the President a substantially higher approval vote.

After a year and a half of what the public quickly came to believe was a "useless war," President Truman's popularity hit its lowest point in his entire administration. In November, 1951, only 23 per cent of the electorate approved of the way Truman was handling his job in office.

During those eighteen months, public opinion polls charted the public's increasing frustration with our inability to come to grips with the real villain in Korea — the Soviet Union. Eight out of ten Americans early in 1951 said they believed that Red China had entered the war directly on orders from Moscow.

Since we were denied the chance to lock horns with our major enemy, we thought the best thing, once the war in Korea looked as if it would drag on without conclusive results, was to get out. As early as January of 1951, two out of three Americans favored our pulling out of Korea.

In the first months of the war, a majority of the public had approved our crossing the 38th parallel and driving up into North Korea. By the spring of 1951, we were ready to split Korea with the Communists along the lines that had existed when the war started. Yet the fighting was to drag on for another two years — years in which American lives continued to be lost. The final result, after all of our trouble, was a division of Korea for which we had been ready to settle early in the war.

During the years of Korea, however, Americans were in no sense giving in to Russia. Throughout this period, the polls recorded continued support for keeping our defenses strong against Communism. It merely seemed that Korea, with the Communist sanctuary north of the Yalu, was not the most appropriate place to do battle with Russia or her allies.

Our reverses in Asia made us become even more "Europe-oriented." Although cautious and critical of becoming involved in a major war in the Far East, Americans were highly in favor of sending troops to Europe to keep our commitment to the NATO alliance. After the disillusionment of Korea, public opinion became even more convinced that the real battle, if it had to come, should be fought face-to-face with the Russians in Europe.

The 2000th anniversary of Paris, celebrated in 1950 and 1951, brought many Americans to that city and spurred more than six out of ten Americans in a Gallup Poll to say they would like some day to visit the French capital. One of the many thousands of Americans who did arrive in Paris in 1951 came to lead the American forces in Europe.

General Dwight D. Eisenhower was a familiar figure to the United States public when he assumed command of NATO. He was picked in 1950 by his fellow Americans as the man whom they most admired in all the world. President Truman was third on the public's list of most admired men that year.

If anything was needed to set the stage for Eisenhower's rise in political popularity, the disappointment and humiliation of Korea could not have been better suited. The long-time suspicion of many voters that President Truman was "not a big enough man for the job" was confirmed by what seemed to be the confused course in Korea. In Eisenhower, voters sensed a man who was big enough for the job they had in mind — the Korean dilemma chiefly served to pinpoint Truman's weaknesses and Eisenhower's strong points.

The fact that Eisenhower appeared to the public to be moving in the direction of the Republicans helped matters. The voters had been coming around to the view that maybe the GOP could do a better job of handling the war effort than the Democrats could. The events in Korea pushed this trend further — if the Chinese Communist invasion had been one month earlier or the 1950 Congressional elections one month later, President Truman might well have had another Republican-controlled Congress to deal with in his last two years in office.

5

The Soldier and the Senator

WITH DWIGHT D. EISENHOWER at the head of the Republican ticket, 1952 was a year when traditional political alignments went by the board. In an electorate where nominal Democrats clearly outnumbered Republicans, the GOP candidate polled some six million more votes than did his Democratic opponent, Adlai Stevenson. Five normally Democratic states of the Solid South gave their electoral votes to Eisenhower. His total popular vote of nearly 34 million was the greatest given any Presidential candidate in history.

For all his obvious popularity with voters, Eisenhower's coattails were not strong enough to bring his party a working margin of seats in Congress. In the House of Representatives, the GOP came out of the 1952 election with only an eight-seat margin; in the Senate there were 48 Republicans, 47 Democrats and one Independent, Wayne Morse, who later turned to the Democrats.

One title that the public would never apply to Eisenhower was that of Mr. Republican. He was consistently a supra-party figure — in that fact lay much of his popular strength. General Eisenhower generated a warm and spontaneous admiration in millions of voters across the country who were more normally Democratic or did not generally bother to vote. Their votes helped swell those from his own party's rank and file to make the record-breaking total. A deep-seated public confidence in Eisenhower's ability to set the country straight enabled him to stem strong political tides which most GOP candidates could not have offset.

Although Eisenhower's candidacy would have had great appeal to the American public at almost any time since the death of Roosevelt, his arrival on the national political

1952 VOTE AND PARTY AFFILIATION

Vote for		*Voters consider themselves*	
Eisenhower	54.9	Republicans	34
Stevenson	44.4	Democrats	39
Other candidates	0.7	Independents	27

scene came at an ideal moment: the inconclusiveness of the Korean war and the growing lack of confidence in President Truman combined with Eisenhower's natural appeal to voters made a dream candidate for the GOP in 1952.

Public opinion poll findings indicate clearly that the public was ready to support Eisenhower overwhelmingly long before he entered the political battle against Senator Robert Taft in 1952. By convention time that summer, the Ike bandwagon had been on the road for some years — it remained only for the professional politicians to allow the voters the opportunity of putting Eisenhower into office.

Looked at purely from a grass roots point of view, the Taft-Ike battles in primary elections in 1952 were only incidental to a race whose outcome was seldom in doubt. At the national level, Eisenhower held a wide lead over Taft throughout the struggle for the nomination.

The primaries in 1952 reflected chiefly the conflicting sentiments within the ranks of the Republican party. Taft united conservative elements in the GOP as no other Republican leader had done since Governor Alfred Landon in 1936. In no public opinion poll since 1936 had any conservative Republican gotten anything like the support Senator Taft enjoyed in the spring of 1952.

Taft was facing, however, what Louis Harris has succinctly described as a "household word." The Senator had to contend with a man who for some years had been as well known as any other living American and who was deeply admired by millions.

In early April of 1952, when the Taft forces were delighting in the primary returns from Wisconsin, Nebraska and Illinois, Gallup Poll reporters across the nation were recording an overwhelming preference for Eisenhower over Democrat Senator Estes Kefauver. In a comparable poll test, Taft ran behind the Tennessee Senator by a sizable margin.

Months before the primaries, public opinion polls had turned up such novel findings about Eisenhower's appeal as one in which he was the first choice of *both* Republicans and Democrats to head their respective tickets in 1952. Another had shown Eisenhower, hypothetically running on a Democratic ticket, handily defeating Taft on the Republican ticket.

Few, if any, personalities have had their public career chronicled by the public opinion polls in such great detail as has Dwight Eisenhower. From the very first, the polls indicated that in Eisenhower the public sensed a potential leader.

Ike's initial appearance in a poll heralded some of the unique appeal he would have to the electorate. In March, 1945, at a time when the armies Eisenhower commanded were closing in on Nazi Germany, the public was asked who they thought was the smartest American general of World War II. Eisenhower ran second to General Douglas MacArthur in that sampling of opinion.

Eisenhower's military ability was never quite the keystone of his political popularity. The Democratic argument that Ike was too military never really got off the ground. MacArthur, the more colorful, the more dashing, was respected by Americans for his ability as a general. Eisenhower, the administrator, the compromiser who kept the alliance together and working, was admired by Americans for his administrative leadership. Harris, in *Is There a Republican Majority?*, writes of this phenomenon:

98

MacArthur was the recipient of people's fears about a military man in the White House. The general from the East was the embodiment of a military man's general to millions of Americans. The people were grateful to him for the service he had rendered the nation. They admired his strength as an individual. But they distrusted him as a political leader. Eisenhower did not evoke the same reaction. If anything, he was better received as a potential President than as a military leader.

As early as the fall of 1945, there was enough speculation about Eisenhower as a potential President to warrant testing his chances against Truman in a Gallup Poll. Ike polled 26 per cent of the vote, Truman — highly popular at the time — 54 per cent, the remainder were undecided. Eisenhower, a practically unknown figure politically, could still pull the support of about one fourth of the electorate from an extremely well-liked Chief Executive. It was the only time that Eisenhower ran this poorly against Truman in poll tests.

Early in 1946, Eisenhower shared top honors with MacArthur as the public's choice of Most Admired Man. President Truman, his popularity fallen below the 50 per cent line, was in third place behind the two generals.

Considering that much of Eisenhower's appeal came from the fact of his being thought of as a replacement for FDR, Ike's early popularity among younger voters — who were only in their teens when Roosevelt last ran for office — is noteworthy. In 1946, he was the fourth-place choice of first voters in both the Republican and Democratic party to head their parties' tickets in 1948. This finding looked ahead to the strength that Eisenhower had in 1952 and 1956 among the younger voters.

As early as 1946 Eisenhower possessed one priceless political advantage — that of being widely known to the public. Two years before Adlai Stevenson became Governor of Illinois, 92 Americans in every 100 knew who Eisenhower was. In a list of prominent personalities in public life, Ike's score was topped only by Bing Crosby's 94 per cent. The nearest to these two household words was Governor Thomas Dewey with an identification score of 75 per cent. Senator Taft was known at the time to only 22 per cent.

From one point of view, Ike was better known than "The Star-Spangled Banner." Only eight voters in a hundred did not know who Eisenhower was. Another poll at about the same time found that twenty-six voters in a hundred did not know the name of our national anthem.

With advantages such as these, Eisenhower's name was figuring in political speculation by late 1946. Nearly four voters in ten in a Gallup Poll said they would like to see the General be a presidential candidate in 1948. Only about half that number, however, actually believed he would run.

Just which political party Eisenhower belonged to, however, was a moot question. When voters were asked with which party they thought the General would ally himself if he did seek the nomination, nearly half said they didn't know. Among those who did venture a guess, it was a toss-up as to whether Ike was a Republican or a Democrat.

100

No matter which party label he might choose, however, the public liked the image they had of Eisenhower — perhaps because it somehow paralleled the image that the voters, collectively, had of themselves. When the public was asked whether they thought the General was a conservative or a liberal, 48 per cent said they didn't know, while the remainder split about evenly between the two. This description of Eisenhower was not unlike the way in which voters described their own political tendencies (or lack of them). The General fitted comfortably into the national political conscience as a sort of electoral Everyman.

PARALLEL IMAGES

	Ike Described as	Voters Describe themselves as
Conservative	27	37
Liberal	25	33
Uncertain	48	30

By early 1947, Eisenhower bulked large in the public's thinking about Presidential candidates. Although he himself commented at about this time that "A man with no party affiliation could not even discuss running for President of the United States," the voters obviously did not agree with Eisenhower's reasoning. His very lack of sharp identification with party, in fact, was the basis for much of his popularity and one of the main reasons why he finally got to be President.

A recheck by the Gallup Poll on what voters thought about Eisenhower's personal politics found the picture in

1947 even more obscure than it had been earlier. Six out of ten voters now said they didn't know what Ike's politics were; the remainder again split between the two parties almost evenly. Yet the percentage wanting him to run in 1948 remained unchanged. Each party's rank and file tended to think of Eisenhower as one of their own, and thus assume he would run on their ticket.

Eisenhower's political potential was seen in another Gallup Poll test run of his chances against Truman in the fall of 1947. The General had now pulled out ahead of President Truman by a comfortable majority of the two-way vote (that is, excluding about one voter in eight who was undecided). More than one fourth of the Democrats in this poll bolted from Truman to vote for Eisenhower — or roughly the same proportion of Democrats who actually did vote for Ike in 1952.

By the time Eisenhower definitely ruled himself out of political consideration in the 1948 campaign, he was the second choice of Republican voters for their party's nomination, just behind Governor Dewey. And he was the first choice of the Independent voters, leading a list of candidate possibilities from both parties.

A test of the strength of both Eisenhower and Taft against Truman showed the President trailing the General, but ahead of the Senator. Ike had an edge in union member support against Truman; Taft was way behind. Both Ike and Taft ran ahead of Truman in farm voting, but the Senator by a somewhat slimmer margin than the General did. Veterans, who gave Truman a heavy margin

STRENGTH OF EISENHOWER AND TAFT — 1948

	All Voters	Union Members	Farmers	Veterans
Eisenhower	54	55	56	55
Truman	46	45	44	45
Taft	38	30	52	35
Truman	62	70	48	65

(Vote excludes Wallace and undecided voters)

over Taft, swung to Eisenhower when he was posed as the GOP candidate.

Some of the basis for Eisenhower's appeal was discussed by Harold Isaacs in *Newsweek* in the spring of 1948. From various poll findings, Isaacs created a hypothetical "Majority Man" and went on to say this about him:

For thirteen years, the Majority Man remained faithful to Franklin D. Roosevelt. Times changed and policies shifted, but the Man followed Roosevelt because, for better or worse, he relied on the Roosevelt judgment and was willing to submit to the Roosevelt leadership. . . .

What he [the Majority Man] is really looking for, as the enthusiasm for Eisenhower has shown, is someone to fill the seat of the Great White Father vacated by Franklin D. Roosevelt, someone to take him by the hand and lead him through the maze of events toward peace and security. By a curious combination of impressions and moods and mental images, he has come to believe that Eisenhower is the man to do it, although neither the Majority Man nor anyone else knows what Eisen-

103

hower thinks in any concrete detail, about the major issues of the moment.

As the Republican high command surveyed the shambles that remained after Truman's 1948 victory, a Gallup Poll asked rank and file members of the GOP what they thought their party needed in order to be revitalized — new leaders or new programs. The desire for new faces won out over new platforms by nearly 2 to 1. Not unsurprisingly, the first test of 1952 GOP possibilities in mid-1949 found a relatively new face high on the list. Eisenhower, still new politically, was in a three-way tie for first place with Dewey and Harold Stassen — each man had about 20 per cent of the GOP vote. Behind the top three trailed MacArthur and Taft.

The question of Eisenhower's personal political preference had begun to clear up, if only slightly. Four voters in ten in 1949 were still undecided as to whether Ike was a Republican or a Democrat. But among those who thought they had guessed his political leanings, a growing number believed he was in the GOP camp. A majority of Republican voters felt this was the case, while Democrats swung from a position of feeling he was a Democrat to being split almost evenly on the issue.

Some non-political signs of the times were offered in other Gallup Poll findings in 1949. In the spring of that year, something like 3 million U.S. adults were estimated to have been swept up in the Pyramid Club craze. Less than half of all persons questioned in a June poll (44 per cent) said they had ever seen a television show. Only about half of America's husbands and wives were certain they would marry the same person again. Bob Hope was named as the funniest comedian on the air, while in a poll of baseball fans Joe DiMaggio was named "The Greatest Player in the Game Today." As the end of the year marked the midpoint of the twentieth century, 63 per cent of Americans foresaw trains and planes run by atomic power in the year 2000, and 88 per cent believed there would be a cure for cancer by that time.

The end of 1949 saw Eisenhower emerge as the first-place choice of Republican voters for the 1952 nomination. Stassen was in second place, Taft in third.

A Gallup Poll in 1949 asked the public for its opinion of Taft and the job he was doing as a Senator. About four persons in ten had no opinion on Taft; among those who did, favorable attitudes outweighed unfavorable ones by about 3 to 2. More important in terms of the political struggle to come, Senator Taft got a resounding endorsement from members of his own party.

In 1949 also, the Ohio Senator was in seventh place as the man living anywhere in the world who was most admired by the American people — a high ranking for a U.S. Senator on a list usually dominated by heads of state, religious personalities, or humanitarian figures. Up in second place, however, just behind President Truman, was Dwight Eisenhower. One year later, Taft had moved up to sixth place, while Eisenhower had nudged Truman out of first.

By the spring of 1950, the list of possible Republican candidates had a rank order that it would pretty much

MOST ADMIRED MEN
(Ranked by order of mentions)

1949	1950
1. Harry Truman	1. Dwight Eisenhower
2. Dwight Eisenhower	2. Douglas MacArthur
3. Winston Churchill	3. Harry Truman
4. Douglas MacArthur	4. Winston Churchill
5. Herbert Hoover	5. Herbert Hoover
6. Pius XII	6. Robert Taft
7. Robert Taft	7. Bernard Baruch
8. Bernard Baruch	8. Pius XII
9. Alben Barkley	9. Ralph Bunche
10. Thomas Dewey	10. Thomas Dewey

hold up to convention time in the summer of 1952. Running first and second with GOP voters were Eisenhower and Taft. At this point, however, the General held about a 20-point lead over the Senator.

The outbreak of war in Korea caused only a slight upswing in Eisenhower's popularity for the Republican nomination. It was not until the fighting there had bogged down into what seemed a fruitless struggle that Ike's underlying strength on this issue would serve his cause. The initial action in Korea actually helped Truman's popularity.

Senator Taft's landslide victory in Ohio in November, 1950, boosted his cause effectively. A winner by a thin 17,000 votes in his home state in 1944, Taft came through with a whopping 437,000 vote margin in his successful re-election try in 1950. This demonstration of vote-getting power, plus the particular appeal to conservative Republicans of Taft's stand on the "useless war," served greatly to rally the right wing of his party. Nor did the endorsement of Eisenhower's candidacy by the liberal Republican Dewey detract from Taft's appeal to conservatives. The pattern of the Taft-Ike struggle was set. At the end of 1950, Eisenhower had the support of roughly one Republican in three, Taft of roughly one in four.

In 1951, Taft was probably better known than any other member of the Senate. If he had a rival on this count, it would have been Tennessee's Estes Kefauver, whose televised investigations of organized crime were widely followed by the public. In the wake of the Kefauver hearings, seven out of ten persons in a Gallup Poll said they would like to have sessions of Congress televised.

Americans had a favorable impression of Taft's performance as a Senator, but many voters were disinclined to think of him as good Presidential timber. Republican voters thought Taft would make a good President; Democrats and Independents were both dubious on this point.

Some of the verbatim replies people gave Gallup Poll reporters give the best idea of what voters thought about Senator Taft. In the favorable department were such comments as: "He is one of the brainiest men in the country today." "Nobody else in the Republican party comes up to him." "He's honest, conscientious, able and 100 per cent American."

In the unfavorable category were statements like this: "He's too narrow, basically an isolationist, although he denies it in one breath and confirms it in the next." "He has no heart, he wouldn't give a darn about anybody in the country except people who influence him." "He isn't colorful enough or big enough to be President."

By way of comparison, Eisenhower showed little in his make-up which alienated any major bloc of voters. If his lack of a stand on all but the broadest of issues failed to identify him with any particular wing or political philosophy, it also kept him from making many political enemies.

In the spring of 1951 came the amazing poll finding that Eisenhower was the top choice of both Republican and Democratic voters for the 1952 nomination. If anything, Ike was slightly more popular with Democrats than he was with GOP voters. He ran farther ahead of Truman in the Democratic test than he did ahead of Taft in the Republican list.

With President Truman's personal popularity hitting bottom in 1951, both of the leading Republican candidates defeated him in polling tests throughout the year. But whereas Eisenhower's margins over Truman were definitely of the landslide variety, Taft's edge was generally

TAFT vs. EISENHOWER — 1951

When Matched Against Truman

	All Voters	Republicans	Democrats	Independents
Eisenhower	68	97	37	80
Truman	32	3	63	20
Taft	52	91	19	51
Truman	48	9	81	49

slim enough to give practical politicians food for thought about what a hard-fought campaign on Truman's part might do to this edge.

Both Eisenhower and Taft had the overwhelming support of members of their own party. Once out of the

Republican ranks, however, the picture changed drastically. About twice as many Democrats broke from Truman to vote for Ike as was true in the case of the Taft-Truman polling match. And where Eisenhower had the overwhelming support of the Independent voters, Taft split the vote of this group almost evenly with Truman.

Within the ranks of the Republican party, however, Taft's popularity for the Presidential nomination was growing. As right-wing resentment over the handling of the Korean war intensified, the Senator pulled up on Eisenhower. By early 1952, the General and the Senator stood dead even in popularity among Republican voters. Taft held this position through the early spring until, coinciding with the first primary returns in March and April, Eisenhower picked up strength once again. From then until convention time, Ike's lead did not diminish.

EISENHOWER-TAFT BATTLE — 1950-1952

Republican Voters' Preferences

	Eisenhower	Taft
December, 1950	35	24
April, 1951	38	22
June	30	22
December	30	28
February, 1952	33	33
March	33	34
April	37	34
May	44	33
Early June	43	36
Late June	44	35
July	46	35

Eisenhower nominated on first ballot in GOP convention, July, 1952, in Chicago.

One thing is clear about the trends of voter sentiment during the course of the Eisenhower-Taft battle. Even within the ranks of the Republican party — except for a period of about four months in early 1952 — the popular choice was generally Eisenhower.

If there was a struggle, it came chiefly between the professional politicians in the Republican party and the GOP rank and file. As part of its coverage of the 1952 nomination fight, the Gallup Poll sounded the views of Republican county chairmen on several occasions. These local party leaders, who often play an important role in the selection of convention delegates, were consistently in favor of Taft's nomination by overwhelming majorities.

Aside from any consideration of who was the better man, the purely political wisdom in nominating Eisenhower is best assessed in terms of how he and Taft scored at a national level where the views of all voters — not just Republicans — are taken into account. Conventions try to select a candidate who they feel will win. In picking Eisenhower over Taft, the GOP delegates went for what then appeared (and later proved) to be a safe bet compared to what was, at best, an uncertain chance.

Could Taft have won in 1952 if he had gotten the nomination? Maybe the question should remain in the "Could Marciano have beaten Dempsey?" category. On the other hand, some speculation is illuminating on this teaser.

Both Taft and Eisenhower had demonstrated an ability to defeat President Truman in poll tests. Eisenhower's margin was always decisive, however, while Taft's, from a pollster's point of view, was close to the margin of error built into all sampling efforts.

A good deal of Taft's strength seems to have been as much an anti-Truman as it was a pro-Taft vote. By the time Truman withdrew from the race in March, 1952, Senator Kefauver had overtaken the President as the popular choice of Democratic voters for their party's nomination. A test of Taft's and Eisenhower's strength against the Tennessee Senator found Ike well ahead, Taft trailing. The pattern of party voting was much the same as it had been against Truman. Both Republicans held their own party's vote; Independents and Democrats broke sharply for Eisenhower, but did not follow for Taft.

TAFT vs. EISENHOWER — 1952

When Matched Against Kefauver

	All Voters	Republicans	Democrats	Independents
Eisenhower	64	87	42	66
Kefauver	36	13	58	34
Taft	47	84	15	42
Kefauver	53	16	85	58

If Senator Taft had been the GOP nominee in 1952, it seems that two of his most logical campaign arguments would have been (1) it's time for a change, and (2) the Democrats are responsible for Korea. In the case of both of these, serious questions arise as to how effectively they might have worked for Taft.

The argument that it was time to throw the Democratic

111

rascals out of office was a kind of simple, easily understood political charge. The fact that the Democrats happened to have been in office for a conveniently round twenty years only made it that much easier to fashion a campaign slogan. If not a particularly emotional issue, it was at least easy to remember.

"It's time for a change" was a reason for voting for Eisenhower that Gallup Poll reporters heard frequently in the 1952 campaign. Yet was it really time to change parties, or just time to change from a Chief Executive in whom the electorate had lost confidence to one with new qualities of leadership? At the Congressional level, there was a shift of only one-tenth of a percentage point to the Republicans between 1950 and 1952.

If it were simply a case of wanting to replace President Truman, a vote for *either* Taft *or* Stevenson — had they opposed each other — would have served the purpose. There is considerable survey evidence to show that growing numbers of voters came to think of Governor Stevenson as an appealing personality during the course of the campaign. Against Eisenhower, Stevenson was battling an immensely popular figure on whom the voters had had their eye for many years. Against Taft, such would not have been the case.

In the case of the Korean argument, it seems likely that Truman's withdrawal from the race removed much of the advantage that Taft might have derived from this issue. Much of the bitterness over Korea was directed at Truman and if the President had been Taft's opponent in 1952, this issue would have been working heavily in the

Senator's favor. Few voters, however, blamed Stevenson specifically for the Korean situation — he just didn't have that much connection with it.

That this issue did not evaporate in Eisenhower's case is a result of the unique position Ike enjoyed as a war hero and military leader. People voted *against* Truman in the public opinion polls because of Korea; they voted *for* Eisenhower (who had pledged to make a personal effort to seek a Korean truce) for the same reason.

Also working against Senator Taft, had he been the Republican nominee, was the fact that as "Mr. Republican" he was the embodiment of a political philosophy repudiated by a majority of the electorate. If Taft's 100 per cent Republicanism could have meant his defeat in 1952, Eisenhower's lack of identification with the GOP played a large part in his victory. The reasons why Taft might not have won are essentially the reasons why Eisenhower did triumph. They are also among the reasons why he was such a highly popular President during his first term in office.

6

Ike — The People's Possession

To MANY MILLIONS OF AMERICANS, President Eisenhower's 1953 inauguration symbolized not so much the coming of a new era in government as it did the re-establishment of an old one in which there was strong leadership in the executive branch. As such, the first Republican administration in twenty years hearkened back to the days of Roosevelt as much as it looked ahead to any brave new political world.

General Eisenhower was more than just the people's choice — he was the people's possession. It was the ordinary voter all across the country who had called for Ike's candidacy in so strong a voice that the politicians could not deny it to him.

To the relief of many a headline writer, the people told Gallup Poll reporters shortly after Eisenhower took office that they had no objection to the President being referred to in print as Ike (there were reservations, however, about Mrs. Eisenhower's being called Mamie). Significantly, perhaps, no such issue had arisen during Truman's administration.

Because he was so much the candidate of the people, Eisenhower brought to the Presidency an enormous, underlying strength. In their deep admiration for the man, voters were willing to overlook Ike's early fumblings in the unfamiliar game of politics. One thing, however, the voters did demand of Eisenhower. That was that he *do something* to prove that the voters had not been wrong in assessing his leadership potential. In this demand lay both Ike's greatest strength — and his greatest weakness.

In charting Eisenhower's personal popularity with voters since 1953, the Gallup Poll has noted two particular areas in which the President could provoke sharp public reaction.

First, the polls noted Ike's particular susceptibility to what columnists liked to call "do-nothing sentiment." The voters didn't call it this; they said Eisenhower was "away too much," or "playing too much golf," or "listening to his advisers too much." What people seemed to be voicing actually was a dissatisfaction with a lack of definite action on the President's part. Generally speaking, the downtrends in Eisenhower's popularity during his first term occurred when do-nothing talk was most prevalent.

Second, sharp upswings in Eisenhower's popularity generally followed some decisive or dramatic action on his part which involved our foreign policy or national

115

security. This reaction can again be traced directly to the reasons why people voted for Ike. He was the military hero on whose wisdom and strength voters could rely.

But Eisenhower was not an up-and-down President, subject to wide fluctuations in his standing with the public. His popularity rating showed a great deal more stability than either Roosevelt or Truman. During his first four years in office, Eisenhower's Gallup Poll popularity averaged 70 per cent; during two thirds of that time his popularity was no more than five percentage points away from the average. By comparison, President Truman, with an average popularity of 46 per cent, was within five points of his average only about one eighth of the time.

President Truman came into office in 1945 as an unknown quantity; moreover, the voters had not personally chosen him. He was in the position of having to prove himself. When Truman appeared to have failed, the public concluded, "The job is too big for the man."

President Eisenhower was well known long before his inauguration and warmly admired by voters in a personal sense — "I Like Ike" was one of the most effective and accurate campaign slogans ever devised. When Ike appeared to have failed in some respects, voters were inclined to blame it on the job. "He's doing as well as can be expected" is a phrase Gallup Poll reporters often heard. It was offered more as an apology for the burden put upon him than as a criticism of the General's shortcomings.

In short, Truman was more often than not "guilty until

proved innocent," Eisenhower, "innocent until proved guilty."

Eisenhower's initial popularity score in the Gallup Poll was 68 per cent — only two points below his first-term average. It remained at about this level through the first few months, then pushed upward following new moves toward the eventual settlement of the cease-fire in Korea. With his administration only six months old, Ike had already achieved one major goal that the public had set for him.

There was criticism from some official circles that summer that the President was playing too much golf. A Gallup Poll found, however, that only 17 per cent of the public shared this sentiment. The vote had partisan overtones; about one Democratic voter in four felt Ike was spending much time on the links. A Lawrence, Massachusetts, laborer commented to a Poll reporter: "Every other day I pick up the paper, he's off on a golf spree."

The fall of 1953 saw the first serious instance of do-nothing sentiment building up. By the end of the year, Eisenhower's popularity had slipped off to 60 per cent, still a majority vote of confidence, but clearly a decline from the summertime satisfaction with the end of the war in Korea.

A Gallup Poll in the summer of 1953 turned up the fact that nearly half (49 per cent) of all American workers had a coffee break at their place of work. Another found that most Americans drove to work by car — spending an average of 18 minutes on the road each morning and evening.

Glimmerings that a popular Republican Chief Executive did not necessarily mean a popular Republican party appeared in the fall of 1953. In New Jersey's Sixth Congressional District, where the GOP had won nearly two thirds of the vote a year earlier, Democrat Harrison Williams was the winner in a special House by-election. In the Ninth District of Wisconsin, Democrat Lester Johnson gained a House seat in what had long been regarded as a solidly Republican district.

The slight downturn in the President's popularity was quickly halted and reversed by his speech before the United Nations in December, 1953, in which he called for international cooperation on the peaceful use of atomic energy. Thanks to Atoms for Peace, Eisenhower's standing with the voters after one year in office was back to where he had started off. This was the first instance of the President's ability to recoup lost ground dramatically with a single, decisive move touching on international harmony.

Then Eisenhower's popularity once again began to fall. The downtrend was occasioned chiefly by the President's seeming to stand off and take no firm position on either the Army-McCarthy hearings or the war in Indo-China. When Dienbienphu fell in May, 1954, Ike's standing with voters was again down near the 60 per cent line. The full-scale political circus featuring the United States Army and Senator Joseph McCarthy in the center ring did not help matters much, particularly when Eisenhower stated at a press conference that he didn't know what the term "McCarthyism" meant.

118

The approaching 1954 Congressional elections brought survey findings which made clear the fact that in any discussion of the political scene, two distinct levels had to be considered. On one level was Eisenhower, a figure on whom the day-to-day political discontent simply did not rub off. On the second level was the partisan struggle between Republicans and Democrats, in which the latter continued to lead by a substantial number. A Gallup Poll in the fall of 1954 asked voters how they would register if forced to sign up again with either of the two major parties. This question, aimed at avoiding purely

IF ALL VOTERS REGISTERED AGAIN — 1954*

	Would Sign Up As	
Democrats	54,600,000
Republicans	35,100,000
On the Fence	7,800,000

*Based on estimated 97.5 million civilian citizens of voting age.

local political pressures such as exist in the one-party South, found that the Democrats outnumbered the Republicans by an estimated 20 million voters.

It was on this second level that the GOP fought and lost the 1954 battle for control of the House of Representatives. Eisenhower's massive personal popularity did not convince voters that his party merited their allegiance. The electorate had completely scrambled party allegiances in voting for Ike; it expected him to put up with this now that he was in office. Many voters in fact thought it was a good idea to have a President of one party and the Congress controlled by another. As one Indiana farmer said:

119

"That way, it kind of keeps them on their toes — one won't let the other get away with anything."

As novel as this reasoning may sound to some political scientists, it was one of the chief reasons why the GOP plea to give Ike a Republican Congress fell so flat in 1954.

For many nominal Democrats who had supported Eisenhower in 1952, their accompanying vote for a Republican Congressman had been very much in the nature of a thirty-day trial. With unemployment on the rise in 1954, many normally Democratic voters felt that the trial period was over and they wanted their money back. A factory worker from Worcester, Massachusetts, reasoned it this way:

"I've always been a Democrat, but I voted for Ike last time. Now a lot of my buddies are out of a job and I'm gonna vote Democratic again. I want to keep my job."

Eisenhower's popularity, of course, did respond to the election fight. It hit its first-term low point in the wake of the Democratic victory. But a substantial majority still approved of the President's performance in office. The 57 per cent approval score of November, 1954, was off only 11 points from the vote when Eisenhower took office. By way of contrast, Truman's popularity at the time of the GOP Congressional victory in 1946 was 32 per cent — 55 points below the approval when he took over the Presidency in 1945.

By early 1955, with an international crisis brewing in the Straits of Formosa, Eisenhower's popularity was back to its inaugural level of 68 per cent — a plateau it maintained through midsummer.

At least some Americans had other things than Formosa on their minds in the spring of 1955. A preoccupation for many was the mambo — some seven million adults, the Gallup Poll estimated, had tried shuffling and shaking to the new Latin American rhythm by early 1955.

We were also reading that spring about the romance between England's Princess Margaret and Captain Peter Townsend. Some 63 per cent of Americans said that if the princess and the captain wished to marry, they should go ahead and do so (virtually the same per cent who had approved of the marriage between the Duke of Windsor and Wallace Simpson nearly twenty years earlier).

Perhaps the most dramatic example of Eisenhower's ability to stir the electorate came in late July of 1955 at the summit conference in Geneva. Ike's performance at the Big Four meeting was apparently just what the public wanted of him. On his return from Europe, the Gallup Poll recorded a ten-point rise in his popularity to an all-time high point of 79 per cent.

Ironically, when a poll put the specifics of the president's "open skies" plan to the American public, the proposals met with reluctance and skepticism. It was seemingly not so much a case of *what* Ike had proposed as it was the fact that he had taken the initiative against the Russians. He had displayed to both the Russians and the United States public the kind of cold war leadership which we felt was needed.

Long before the President's heart attack in the fall of 1955, there had been considerable speculation about the Republicans' 1956 chances in the event Eisenhower chose not to run again. The GOP outlook was pessimistic. No other leading Republican except Chief Justice Earl Warren came even close to Ike's vote potential against the Democrats. And Warren, in the spring of 1955, had definitely taken himself out of the race. Vice-President Richard Nixon was trailing both Stevenson and Kefauver in Gallup Poll test contests. Senate Minority Leader William F. Knowland and Presidential Assistant Harold Stassen ran an even poorer race against the top Democrats. Warren's withdrawal thus left the Republicans with no strong contender in the event Eisenhower was not able to run. All of which helps to explain why, once recuperation seemed a sure thing, the question of the President's candidacy, as Robert Donovan puts it in *Eisenhower, The Inside Story,* "instead of being preposterous was monopolizing attention."

On the eve of the President's announced decision to seek re-election in 1956, the Gallup Poll found his popularity rating only slightly below that he enjoyed on his return from Geneva. While Ike had been restricted to his Denver hospital suite and through his convalescence at Gettysburg, the American people's immense admiration held firm. Even with his Presidential duties sharply limited while he rested at Gettysburg, 75 per cent of the public approved of the way he was handling the Presidency. Any Democratic hopes of using the "part-time President" charge effectively should have wilted before this display of confidence.

Affection for a part-time Ike, however, did not mean voter support for full-time Republicanism. In 1954, the electorate had tried out the combination of a Republican Eisenhower and a Democratic Congress. By 1956, two years of this kind of divided government had shown voters that such a combination seemed to be working. The electorate had discovered a constitutional way in which they could have their cake and eat it too; they could vote for Eisenhower *and* vote Democratic. It might be ticket-splitting; it was also the answer to political frustration for millions of U.S. voters.

The 1956 Presidential campaign was one of the quietest in the nation's history. Eisenhower's candidacy had near unanimous support from Republicans. In the rival camp, Stevenson had been the first choice of Democratic voters in every Gallup Poll test since 1952. The harmony of the 1956 nominating conventions only served to emphasize the inevitability of a rerun between the 1952 contenders. Except for John Kennedy in Chicago and Joe Smith in San Francisco, the convention halls were relatively free of excitement.

In the subsequent campaign, Gallup Poll reporters found everywhere a general apathy about the issues. On a late October day in Pittsburgh, to cite just one example, a Gallup Poll reporter working there heard not one mention by those he interviewed of the fact that Eisenhower was coming into town that day for a one-night stand.

Surprisingly, this did not lessen interest in getting to the voting booth. It seemed more a case of voters having already decided which man they would support; the campaigning did little to change their minds. Gallup Polls in the 1956 campaign found virtually no change in the electorate's preferences from the conventions until the last few days, when events in Hungary and Suez changed the political picture swiftly.

Even more than in 1952, the 1956 contest for many voters came down to a choice between a man, Eisenhower, and a party, the Democrats. Time and time again people talked to Gallup Poll reporters about why they were voting for Eisenhower or why they believed the Democrats would look out for their interests best. Rarely did voters express either a glowing admiration for the Democratic *candidate* or a spirited defense of the Republican *party*.

During the 1956 campaign, the Gallup Poll made a series of studies which attempted to get at the *why* behind the preferences of various groups in the electorate. In most groups this pattern of Eisenhower versus the Democrats emerged clearly.

The Supreme Court's desegregation decision in 1954 had focused political attention on the Northern Negro vote. Gallup Poll reporters noted a tendency among Negro voters to speak of *Eisenhower* when they were praising the GOP and to talk about the *Republicans* when they were damning it. Many were clearly torn between the Eisenhower personality and the party of Roosevelt. The comment of one Philadelphian was typical:

"I'd like to see Ike win," he told a Gallup Poll reporter, "but the Democrats have done the most for us. Roosevelt has done a lot for the Negroes and Truman has done a pretty good deal too. I'm sort of in betwixt and between right now."

On Election Day, the appeal of the Democratic party

was strong enough to hold the bulk of Northern Negroes. A few did switch — about one in every eight who had voted Democratic in 1952. Those who did swing over were moved largely by their admiration for the man Eisenhower and not by any great confidence in the Republican party.

Another group whose opinions the Gallup Poll sought were the "egghead voters." Because of the formation in 1956 of the Committee of Arts and Sciences for Eisenhower, there was interest as to the opinions of the country's intellectuals on the race.

There is certain to be disagreement about just what constitutes an egghead. When the term first appeared in Joseph Alsop's column (having been coined by his brother John), it was followed by the question: "But how many eggheads are there?" No one, of course, can say with any precision; or place tight social or economic boundaries on such a group. The Gallup Poll did, however, interview a sample of individuals from the egghead's natural environment — the fields of education, science and arts.

These "opinion leaders,"* asked how they would define the term "egghead," came up with some colorful descriptions:

> Bald inside his cranium as well as outside . . . A muddle-headed intellectual . . . A well-meaning, but overly

*A secret mail ballot was sent to a sample of "opinion leaders" in the fields of education, science and the arts whose names were drawn systematically for *Who's Who in America*. In addition, personal interviews with college faculty members were conducted by Gallup Poll reporters in the Eastern and Midwestern states.

fanatical, sort of impractical "do-gooder" . . . A left-wing crackpot . . . A self-styled "intellectual," full of social science, self-importance and syntax . . . Anyone who disagrees with Charlie Wilson . . . An underpaid educator . . . a Cranium filled with unhatched ideas . . . Scrambled semantics with the sunny side down.

The one definition that met with the widest acceptance from the eggheads was that of "intellectual."

Despite the supposed previous association with Stevenson, the intellectuals interviewed in 1956 showed little inclination toward uniting solidly behind him. Eisenhower actually had a majority of the vote among those interviewed.

More interesting than the mere political line-up, in many ways, were the reasons for voting either Democratic or Republican. Generally speaking, the argument on the Republican side was related to the candidate; on the Democratic side, it was related to party. In short, the egghead vote was motivated by many of the same views that Poll reporters heard when talking with Northern Negro voters.

Republican intellectuals talked mainly about the personality of Eisenhower. Rarely did they refer to basic Republican policies. Democratic eggheads, on the other hand, seldom mentioned the candidate. Their reasons for voting Democratic were usually because of things they thought "the party" would do. They admired Stevenson's intellectuality, but it did not seem to be playing a large part in their decision.

Other groups in the electorate drew this same basic

distinction. Younger voters, for example, were torn between the Democratic tradition in which they were raised and the appeal of Eisenhower. Labor union members liked Ike, but had a hard time forgetting the fact that the Democrats were considered the friends of labor. Even as traditionally a Republican group as Midwestern farmers had, by 1956, come to feel that the Democratic party had their best interests at heart. They too were in conflict between the economic security seemingly offered by the Democrats and the attractive personality offered by Eisenhower.

In this contest of man versus party, the Republican ticket, in a purely political sense, profited by the revolt in Hungary and the war over Suez which erupted only a few days before the election. With neither party given the opportunity to formulate a policy on what the United States should do in the case of Hungary or Suez before Election Day, many Americans felt they had no choice but to put their trust in Eisenhower to handle the situation. An additional three to four million votes in all went to the Republican ticket in the closing days of the campaign after the outbreak of the Hungarian revolution and the Anglo-French invasion of Suez. These changed the Republican margin from a comfortable edge into an overwhelming landslide. Behind the swing to the GOP, a postelection analysis by the Galllup Poll revealed, was the confidence these voters had in Eisenhower's ability to resolve America's position in the international crisis.

Even in the closing days, however, the basic conflict for many voters between the Democratic party and the

TREND OF VOTE IN 1956 CAMPAIGN

	August	September	Early October*	November Election
Eisenhower	52	52	51	57.8
Stevenson	41	41	41	42.2
Undecided	7	7	8	—

*Before Hungary and Suez

GOP candidate was unresolved. It was not until the early morning hours of the day after election that the decision of the electorate became clear. Eisenhower was back in office, by a plurality of nearly 10 million votes. The Democrats would still control Congress, for another two years — and by a slightly bigger margin. The President started his second term faced with an electorate which clearly liked him (his Gallup Poll popularity was at an all-time high of 79 per cent in January, 1957), but just as clearly rejected his party.

7

Joe Must Go — Somewhere

THE GAVEL BANGED DOWN, the last of more than two million words were put into the record, and in a small town in eastern Pennsylvania on June 17, 1954, a bartender flicked off the television set. The two-month-long drama that had millions of Americans as its audience faded into a small pinpoint of light. "Now — maybe my wife will talk to me again," said the bartender, grinning.

His words were a good comment on the state of public opinion at the close of the Army-McCarthy hearings. In many ways, they can also serve as the people's epitaph to the career of the controversial junior Senator from Wisconsin. Although the McCarthy story was to meander on for some six months more until his censure by the Senate, the beginning of the end, from the point of view of public reaction, came with the last verbal jockeying in the gaudy fight between the Wisconsin Senator and the United States Army.

After almost two hundred hours of televised coverage of the hearings, the public was groggy, bewildered — and, above all, bored. Like the bartender, a great many Americans were happy that it was finally over. Typical sentiment was that heard from one voter on the day after the hearings: "An awful expense to taxpayers not amounting to one damn thing." From about the middle of 1954, Gallup Poll checks began to find a growing number of Americans who were indifferent or neutral toward McCarthy.

Before this, however, the public went through a period in which large segments of the population chose up sides to a degree rarely seen outside a national election. Richard Rovere has expressed his concern, in *Senator Joe McCarthy*, over the fact that at one point some 50 per cent of the public in a Gallup Poll held a favorable opinion of the Senator — the zenith of his popularity. Equally remarkable perhaps is the fact that at the low point of his career, only 51 per cent of the public looked unfavor-

McCARTHY'S POPULARITY — HIGH AND LOW POINTS, 1954

	Favorable Opinion	Unfavorable Opinion	No Opinion
January	50	29	21
August	36	51	13

ably on McCarthy. He never succeeded in selling more than half of Americans on his crusade; by the same token, he never completely alienated more than half by his actions. In this is the foundation of the controversy surrounding McCarthy.

At one point, before interest in McCarthy began to wane, an estimated 90 million Americans were ready to express an opinion about him — either pro or con. The public's unusual interest in one Senator was all the more remarkable when one considers how brief was his appearance on the national scene. He first aired his charges about Communists in the State Department in February, 1950. By the end of 1954, he had pretty much ceased to exist as an object of widespread public interest.

His appearance before anything like a full quorum of American public opinion was even more brief. As late as August, 1951, two out of three persons in a Gallup Poll could not tell you who McCarthy was. It was not until early 1953, when 65 per cent of the public had formed an opinion about him, that it was possible to keep any kind of a nationwide check on his popularity. From that point on, the McCarthy story was one of the liveliest ever covered by the public opinion polls.

By the time McCarthy arrived on the scene, the American people had been suffering from a sense of frustration for some years at our being unable to come to grips with our perplexing cold war enemy, Russia. The first few weeks of the Korean fighting gave us only momentary opportunity to relieve these frustrations; the ensuing months of what came to seem a hopeless struggle only built them up again more strongly than ever. Certainly the cease-fire negotiated in Korea caused a national sigh of relief. By the very nature of the terms, however, it lacked the fight to the finish quality which the American character likes so dearly.

131

McCarthy's cause — which took as its alleged target Communism within the country — was endorsed by many because of the threat Communism offered the nation from without. We had not been able to win in Korea; maybe we could achieve some sort of victory in the State Department. A stand against the Reds somewhere was what was desired by many.

Some flavor of the atmosphere in which McCarthy's cry of "Who promoted Peress?" struck a responsive chord is offered by Gallup Poll findings in the months preceding the case of the Army dentist with a suspected Communist background who had been promoted to major.

Two out of three persons in November, 1953, said they would not want a person known to favor Communism to make a speech in their community. Earlier that year, about the same majority indicated that they would not want former members of the Communist party to teach in colleges and universities.

The public was concerned about the Communist threat — but not hysterical about it. They voted down, for example, the suggestion by Representative Harold Velde in 1953 that there was a need for an investigation of Communist infiltration into the ranks of the nation's clergy.

In Samuel Stouffer's *Communism, Conformity and Civil Liberties* — based on one of the most comprehensive public opinion surveys ever taken (the field work was conducted jointly by the Gallup Poll and the National Opinion Research Center) — there is clear evidence that the people, in the spring of 1954, had little deep-seated fear of the Communists taking over the United States from within. There was worry, but not neurotic trembling. When Americans were asked about what was worrying them most, only one in a hundred volunteered that they feared a Red take-over from within. Stouffer goes on in one chapter's summary:

> The international Communist threat, perhaps, like the threat of organized crime, is not directly felt as personal. It is something one reads about and talks about and even sometimes gets angry about. But a picture of the average American as a person with the jitters, trembling lest he find a Red under the bed, is clearly nonsense.

What *was* bothering the American people in late 1953 and early 1954 was the fact that our elected national leaders, over the past decade, had not shown themselves capable of meeting the threat offered by international Communism.

When the Harry Dexter White case broke in late 1953, it only revived some of the bitterness toward President Truman which the public had felt during the Korean War. When Attorney General Herbert Brownell asserted that Truman had given White an important government post in 1946, despite an FBI report that White was spying for Russia, the public tended to side with Brownell more than with Truman in the controversy that ensued:

At the root of the public's support for Brownell was anti-Truman sentiment. It was not that people impugned Truman's loyalty — there was much indignation in certain quarters at the idea of a former President being subpoenaed (a subpoena later dropped). But the White case seemed a confirmation of the fears of many people that our fight against Communism had been at times inept and fumbling. The prevailing public sentiment was that Truman's actions had reflected indecision. And indecision on acting toward Russia and Communism was exactly what the public disliked.

Eisenhower also suffered from the fact that people thought he wasn't decisive enough. If there was as much danger from Communism as someone like McCarthy claimed, the people reasoned, why didn't their Chief Executive step in and do something about this?

Throughout the fall of 1953, as the McCarthy charges multiplied, the President's popularity was trending downward and the first "do-nothing" talk about Eisenhower was in evidence both in the public press and in the public opinion polls. The President's popularity spurted up as a result of his UN speech in December, then trailed off again through the first half of 1954. At a time when the public would doubtless have welcomed some kind of a statement on McCarthy by the President — either pro or con — he offered nothing.

Some of the dissatisfaction with Eisenhower's lack of decision presumably carried over into a satisfaction with McCarthy's definite stand on the Communism issue. No matter how wild and free-swinging the Senator might be, it appeared to some voters that somebody in a position of importance was taking up the fight. If McCarthy chose to fight here at home rather than on international battlefronts, he was at least doing something — something that the voters had expected of Eisenhower.

Obviously, there were probably few specific cases where this transferral of allegiance from Eisenhower to McCarthy was clear-cut. Such things generally happen at an emotional level where the average voter is hard put to verbalize his reasoning. But a look at the sources of McCarthy's public support indicates that something like this was going on in some voters' minds during late 1953 and through the first half of 1954.

From the Gallup studies of January and June, 1954, two separate wings within the ranks of the pro-McCarthyites were defined. Like the wings of a political party, these two groups were not always clearly delineated; many of the pro-McCarthy voters fell partially into one wing, partially into the other.

One wing was composed of persons whose support of McCarthy was based primarily on the fact that he was anti-Communist. People in this group — often professional or business people with college educations — were sometimes repelled by the Senator's high-handed and ruthless tactics. But they backed him, nonetheless, and their chief justification for doing so was often summed up by the question — "Well, he's against Communism, isn't he?"

The second wing liked McCarthy as much for his methods as they did for his anti-Communism. These were persons — many from the working classes and with grade school educations — who admired McCarthy because he

McCARTHY — THE MAN AND HIS METHODS
January, 1954

Opinion of McCarthy Personally

	All Voters	College	High School	Grade School
Approve	50	49	53	45
Disapprove	29	44	28	22
No Opinion	21	7	19	33

Opinion of McCarthy's Methods

	All Voters	College	High School	Grade School
Approve	38	33	39	41
Disapprove	47	60	47	37
No Opinion	15	7	14	22

was "a fighter" and "had the guts to stand up to them." Significantly, the "them" was often an unidentified target. To this wing, *what* McCarthy was fighting against was often not as important as the simple fact of his fighting. They liked the rough-speaking, tough-acting man who seemed to cut through all the pretense and pomposity of official Washington. One factory fireman in Mystic, Connecticut, felt that "you can't use kid gloves for that kind of stuff" (just what he meant by "that kind of stuff" was never made clear). A piano tuner from East Stroudsburg, Pennsylvania, after stating that the Senator might be "a bit radical," went on to comment: "But McCarthy's OK — he's got spunk. They've never pinned a thing on him and he's never been made a fool of." This was shortly after the close of the Army-McCarthy hearings.

During the course of his fight with the Army, McCarthy lost ground generally with voters across the country. His sharpest losses, however, tended to come from persons who would fall into the first, or anti-Communist, wing. He lost fewer friends among the second wing — when the hearings were over, Joe was still the fighter who had "stood up to them" to many in this wing.

McCARTHY LOSES SUPPORT JANUARY-JUNE, 1954

Approving of McCarthy

	All Voters	College Voters	High School Voters	Grade School Voters
January	50	49	53	45
June	34	32	36	33
Loss	16	17	17	12

"Nothing remotely like the Army-McCarthy hearings," Rovere observes, "had ever been seen in American history." The hearings grew out of the charges by the Army that McCarthy and his chief counsel, Roy Cohn, had used improper methods to get preferential treatment for G. David Schine, Army private, a former member of McCarthy's investigating staff. The Senator countercharged that the Army had tried to block him from investigating Communist activities at Fort Monmouth, New Jersey, and the fight was on — in one of the giddiest, gaudiest shows ever put on for the American people.

As the televised sessions got under way, the Gallup Poll estimated that some 78 million Americans were familiar with the basic charges in the dispute. Near the end of the hearings, upwards of 85 million people were following the sessions by television, radio or in their newspapers. An estimated 45 million Americans had seen part of the proceedings on television. It was in every sense of the word a national show.

AUDIENCE FOR McCARTHY-ARMY HEARINGS
By 25th Day of Hearings

Read about in newspapers	65 million adults
Listened to on radio	55 million adults
Watched on television	45 million adults

In the early stages of the hearings, the public's sympathies were with the Army by a ratio of 2 to 1. Throughout the next two months, the Gallup Poll consistently recorded the American people as basically more friendly to the Army than to McCarthy. Yet agreement with the

ARMY vs. McCARTHY

Public agrees more with	Start of hearings	End of hearings
Army	46	40
McCarthy	23	25
Undecided	31	35

cause of Secretary Robert Stevens in principle did not necessarily mean that the public felt the Army was getting its point over. Throughout the hearings, the Army lost ground in terms of the people's judgment on whether or

THE ARMY LOSES ITS CASE
Did Stevens and Adams Use Improper Means?

(Trend among those expressing opinion)

	Start of hearings	Midpoint	End of hearings
Yes	34	47	54
No	66	53	46

not Stevens and his legal counsel, John Adams, had actually used improper means in trying to stop McCarthy from investigating at Fort Monmouth. The sentiment at first was that the Army's methods had been justified. By the end of the hearings, it had flipped over to the other side.

If the Army lost public support on this count, McCarthy did not gain correspondingly — one good reason why the public, at the end of the hearings, took the view of "a plague on both your houses" and felt, in many instances, that the long sessions had been a waste of money. The McCarthy forces went into the hearings with the public believing that the Senator and Cohn had used improper means in trying to get special treatment for Schine; when the hearings were over, sentiment had changed a little.

McCARTHY MAKES NO HEADWAY
Did McCarthy and Cohn Use Improper Means?

(Trend among those expressing opinion)

	Start of hearings	Midpoint	End of hearings
Yes	70	71	68
No	30	29	32

Where the Wisconsin Senator did lose heavily, however, was with those Americans whose support of him was based chiefly on his stand against Communism. This is an impressionistic judgment — but one made after a careful review of various survey findings. In the great welter of televised claims and counterclaims about such things as cropped photos, many of McCarthy's anti-Com-

139

munists came to the conclusion that their man was perhaps not all that dedicated to ridding the United States
of the Red menace. They probably did not move to a
position of outright opposition to the Senator, but chances
are that a growing proportion thereafter were found in
the No Opinion category of Gallup Poll surveys.

In contrast, there was little reason really for those in
the other wing of the McCarthy camp to desert Joe. His
performance had been good from their point of view, he
had continued to show that he was a man who would not
don kid gloves under any circumstances. There were
thus still a good many who admired the Senator for these
reasons after the hearings were over. A New England
barber summarized his reaction: "McCarthy did OK.
He was as calm as a cucumber, he never got excited and
he came right to the point. He had an answer for everything."

With the end of the hearings, McCarthy's days in the
center stage of American public opinion were numbered.
By November, 1954, the major change in a Gallup Poll
was a sharp increase in the No Opinion vote. The Watkins
Committee, which was studying the question of whether
or not the Senate should censure McCarthy, stirred up
far less public interest than the more colorful fight with
the Army. Less than six voters in ten (55 per cent) said
they were familiar with the proceedings of the Watkins
Committee; nine in ten (89 per cent) had followed the
Army-McCarthy hearings.

Newspaper readers at this time may have been more
interested in such Gallup Poll findings as one which dis-

closed that an estimated 32 million men and 10 million women had gone swimming in the nude at some point in their lives. Or that 29 million men and 18 million women had stayed out all night on a party. Or that 9½ million wives admitted to having hit their husband at some point in their marriage while only 8½ million men had retaliated.

Among those Americans who were following the Watkins Committee hearings, the weight of sentiment was that the Senate should censure McCarthy. Persons who had gone to college were 2 to 1 in favor of; those with only grade school educations were evenly divided.

SHOULD SENATE CENSURE McCARTHY?

	All Voters	College Voters	High School Voters	Grade School Voters
Should	44	55	43	37
Should not	35	28	37	37
Undecided	21	17	20	26

A question which often arises in post-mortems on McCarthy centers on how much political power — real or potential — the Senator ever wielded at the national level. The matter of just how many votes he could swing at the national level is perhaps the best measure of how strongly the pro-McCarthy tides were running in the years he was on the scene.

There were several indications in 1954 of what McCarthy's support might mean to a candidate. In the Illinois Senatorial primary, Joseph Meek won the GOP nomination in a field of nine candidates. Meek, who had gone on record with complimentary remarks about McCarthy's exposés, was defeated in November by Senator Paul Douglas. In the Maine Senatorial campaign, Robert Jones had the support of McCarthy, but Margaret Chase Smith defeated Jones in the primary, and went on to victory in the fall.

Gallup Poll findings on a national level supported what is suggested in these state races. In January, 1954, those voters who said they might be influenced by the Senator's endorsement of a candidate were split on the effect this might have; about half said it would make them more likely to vote for this candidate, about half said less likely. Most of those interviewed, however, claimed that such an endorsement wouldn't affect their vote. By the midpoint of the Army-McCarthy hearings, the number of voters who said they would be unaffected by McCarthy's endorsement of a candidate was still large — although down from the January figure. Among those who said this would affect their vote, the Senator's support was thought of much more as a liability than as an asset.

IF McCARTHY ENDORSED A CANDIDATE

	Jan., 1954	May, 1954
Would be more likely to vote for candidate	21	17
Would be less likely to vote for candidate	26	43
Would make no difference, or no opinion	53	40

Rovere reports that McCarthy once told a friend that he expected to "end up either in the White House or in jail." It is unlikely that any but his most bitter opponents had any real desire to see McCarthy behind bars. On the other hand, few of his supporters, judging by polling data, ever really seriously considered him as Presidential timber.

The Gallup Poll tested McCarthy's potential as a White House contender on three different occasions — in January, 1954, at the end of 1954, and then in 1955, when he had pretty much fallen into public obscurity.

In all three of these contests, in which McCarthy was entered as a third-party candidate against Eisenhower on the Republican ticket and Stevenson on the Democratic ticket, the Senator's popular support was virtually identical — about 5 per cent of the total vote. It was a vote centered in neither of the two major parties nor with Independents. About the same proportion of Republicans, Democrats and Independents supported McCarthy. Most of the vote, however, came from groups who would normally have supported Eisenhower. In other polls at

McCARTHY FOR PRESIDENT?

Voters' Preferences	Jan., 1954	Dec., 1954	May, 1955
Eisenhower, Republican	51	51	55
Stevenson, Democrat	35	41	37
McCarthy, Third Party	5	5	4
Undecided	9	3	4

the same time, Stevenson's vote in a two-way contest (just he and Eisenhower) was about the same as his vote in the three-way tests.

This says a lot about the nature of McCarthy's support — it came largely from voters who would normally have supported Eisenhower. If many Americans approved of the Senator at certain points, it was not primarily because of what he was. It was more a case, it seems, of his offering something which was wanted, at a time when nobody else on the national scene made the same offer.

8

Where the Grapes of Wrath Are Stored

IN AMONG THE STATELY MANSIONS in one section of Charleston, South Carolina, is a scattering of run-of-the-mill houses recently converted into apartments. In the second floor, a young white man patiently explained his views to a Gallup Poll reporter:

"Now, look, let's put it this way," he reasoned, "suppose I was to be in a place where there was only one bed for the night between myself and a colored boy. Now I wouldn't sleep in the same bed with him, but I *would* flip a coin with him for the bed. Now, if that isn't fair, what in the hell is?"

If crudely put, the white South's case for separate but equal was nonetheless clearly stated by this young Carolinian. It is a position that much of the white South hopes to be able to maintain. In this man's conviction that he treated Negroes fairly can be seen many of the reasons why many Southern whites reacted as they did to the 1954 Supreme Court ruling on school integration. It seems unlikely that this young Southerner would have participated in the mob violence outside Central High School in Little Rock in September, 1957. It is equally doubtful, had he been there, that he would have actively opposed what happened. Like many Southern whites, he would have deplored the violence, but still supported in principle the basic reasons which brought it about. This chapter deals mainly with the white South's reaction to the 1954 ruling; the next covers the Negro viewpoint.

On the surface, the Supreme Court's ruling provoked a split in public opinion reminiscent of that which existed a century ago in the Civil War. Underneath, however, there have been areas where Southern whites could find agreement from many white persons in the North.

When the Supreme Court ruled unanimously in May, 1954, that racial segregation in the public schools was unconstitutional, a Gallup Poll soon after found that a substantial majority of Americans supported the principle of the ruling. The turbulent years since then have done little to shake the conviction of this majority.

OPINIONS ON SUPREME COURT RULING

— Nationwide —

	Approve	Disapprove	No Opinion
June, 1954	54	41	5
May, 1955	56	38	6
February, 1956	57	38	5
January, 1957	63	31	6
August, 1957	58	36	6
September, 1957	56	38	6
October, 1957	59	35	6
July, 1959	59	35	6

But from the very first the public has had misgivings about the practical working out of integrated schools — particularly under conditions that exist in at least some parts of the South. These misgivings have not been limited to the people of the South. In a number of instances, Northerners have shown themselves far from ready to support a policy of full speed ahead on integration.

The Gallup Poll has also consistently recorded a substantial minority of persons in the North which opposes, even in principle, racial integration in the schools. This body of opinion, made up overwhelmingly of white persons, has remained relatively constant since 1956. About one fourth of all voters outside of the South fit into this category.

HOW NORTHERNERS FEEL ABOUT COURT RULING

Combined Cross-section of Whites and Negroes

	Approve	Disapprove	No Opinion
June, 1954	64	30	6
February, 1956	71	24	5
September, 1957	70	24	6
July, 1959	72	23	5

Even among Northerners who do support the Court ruling, there is often a kind of approval which can only be described as superficial. The endorsement involves nothing immediate or close to home. It is something removed from personal contact — as such, it can be safely approved without fear of the consequences. There is often a lack of emotional conviction which characterizes some

147

voters' approval of integration; by way of contrast there is generally an obvious depth of feeling evident in disapproval of the Court ruling.

There are relatively few areas in the South today where Negroes outnumber whites.* At the time of the Civil War there were three white persons for every two colored; in the latest estimates, whites outnumber Negroes by about three to one. In the 1950 Census, only one county in eight in the Southern states had more than 50 per cent Negro. Not one of the major metropolitan areas in these states had more than half of its population Negro. Yet opposition to integration — in both North and South — has often stemmed from the fear that it might mean that whites would be overwhelmed by colored.

On several occasions the Gallup Poll has asked Northern white parents how much, in effect, their tolerance would be tempered by the number of Negroes attending their children's school. The results are revealing.

In 1958, for example, white parents of school-age children in the North were asked how they would feel about sending their children to a school where only a few of the pupils were Negro. An overwhelming majority had no objection — some, in fact, were doubtless sending their children already to such a school. When asked how they would feel about a school where half of the pupils were Negro, the number of parents objecting tripled. And when a further question was asked about a situation

*In dividing the country into four major regions, the Gallup Poll counts these thirteen states as making up the South: Virginia, North Carolina, South Carolina, Georgia, Florida, Alabama, Mississippi, Louisiana, Texas, Oklahoma, Arkansas, Tennessee and Kentucky.

148

NORTHERN WHITE PARENTS VIEW INTEGRATION
September, 1958

View on sending children to school where

	Few children are Negro	Half are Negro	Over half are Negro
No objections	86	56	36
Would object	13	39	58
Don't know	1	5	6

where colored children outnumbered whites, a majority said they would object to this.

Considering that most of these objecting parents favored the Supreme Court ruling in principle, does this constitute Northern hypocrisy? Possibly it does, but Gallop Poll reporters have often noted that some of the most ardent segregationists in the South are newly arrived Northerners. And roughly four out of ten Northerners in a 1957 Gallup Poll admitted that if they lived in the South they would probably favor segregation.

The number of Negroes in the school made less difference to Southern white parents when they were asked the same series of questions. Three out of four were opposed to the idea of sending their children to a school where even a few students were Negro. Needless to say, the opposition when the proportion of colored students was higher reached even larger dimensions. It is noteworthy that one out of four Southern white parents had no objection to sending their children to school with "a few" Negro pupils.

There is little to indicate that the typical white South-

SOUTHERN WHITE PARENTS VIEW INTEGRATION
September, 1958

View on sending children to school where

	Few children are Negro	Half are Negro	Over half are Negro
No objections	26	15	11
Would object	72	81	84
No opinion	2	4	5

erner has had much change of heart about the principle
of integration since the 1954 Court ruling. If he admits

HOW SOUTHERNERS FEEL ABOUT COURT RULING
Combined Cross-section of Whites and Negroes

	Approve	Disapprove	No Opinion
June, 1954	24	71	5
May, 1955	20	73	7
February, 1956	22	72	6
January, 1957	27	67	6
*October, 1957	23	72	5
July, 1959	22	71	7

*After Little Rock

that integration will probably come to the South some
day, it is an admission he often makes with bitterness. It
is frequently accompanied by the comment that such a
move will not come from within the South. The South's
Negroes are not to blame, as he often reasons it, they
have been stirred up by some outside force made up in
varying proportions of Yankees, the NAACP and even, at
times, the Communist party.

150

If integration of a limited sort is accepted by the white South, it is primarily because such a course is seen as a lesser evil than that of closed schools. It does not mean that the white Southerners like mixed schools — their opposition to the Supreme Court's decision was just as marked in 1959, as in 1954.

During the years in which Montgomery, then Clinton, and finally Little Rock came to be names symbolizing the South's problem, all indications from two special Gallup Poll studies — one early in 1956, the second late in 1957 — are that the gap between the two races widened. The white South during these turbulent years stiffened its resistance to the idea of integration. Southern Negroes closed their ranks tighter than ever.

Just how far apart the two races had grown by late 1957 can be sensed in typical comments from a white person and a Negro, both residing in Mobile, Alabama. A white woman, the wife of a spray painter, told a Gallup Poll reporter: "I just think that God intended no mixing of the races. The Negroes around here are pushing themselves in with the whites — I just don't know how we're going to work this thing out."

Not many blocks away, a Negro store owner told a Gallup Poll reporter at about the same time: "The Negro schools just don't have the equipment that white schools have. And the white people here think Negroes are not up to par with them. It makes me mad. I just don't know how we're going to do this thing. I hope the people will obey the decision."

When the results of the two studies were compared,

it was evident that there had been no increase among white Southerners in pro-integration sentiment over the two-year period. If anything, there was even greater determination in white Southern sentiment that "white and colored just *shouldn't* mix."

THE UNCHANGING WHITE SOUTH
Views on Supreme Court Decision

	Approve	Disapprove	No Opinion
February, 1956	16	80	4
December, 1957	15	83	2

When talking to many white persons practically anywhere in the South, one quickly discovers the conviction, instilled since childhood, that the white man and the black man exist on two entirely separate planes and that it would be wrong to try to change this. All of the arguments thrown up in recent years about states' rights, self-determination and nullification have had their roots in this widespread Southern belief.

Behind this belief are a mixture of religious, cultural, traditional and moral reasons. In some instances these are reinforced by a fear of the trouble and violence that "mixing" the races might cause. This is occasionally accompanied by a sincere protest against what is felt to be a violation of the Constitution. But the feeling that there is something inherently wrong in "mixing" Caucasian and Negro is far and away the reason cited most frequently by white people as a basis for their opposition to integration. The view of a middle-aged addressograph operator from Birmingham is typical:

"It isn't good nor right for black and white to mix," he told a Gallup Poll reporter, "they are two entirely different races. Their habits and their speech and, most important, their morals are different. I work around colored and I understand them. I respect them, but I know they must not be allowed to mix."

The degree of Southern opposition to the Supreme Court decision has been generally related to the size of the Negro population. This calls to mind the voting patterns in the 1948 Dixiecrat revolt, when the areas with the greatest proportions of Negroes tended to turn in heavy votes for the States' Rights ticket.

In the border states of Kentucky, Tennessee, Oklahoma and Texas, for example, where the ratio averages eight whites to one colored, the Gallup Poll in early 1956 found about three out of four whites disapproving of the Supreme Court's ruling. In Florida, Virginia, Arkansas and North Carolina — where Negroes constitute, on the average, about 24 per cent of the total population — there was an upturn in the disapproval vote; about eight whites in ten there opposed the Supreme Court decision. And in the deep South — Georgia, Alabama, Louisiana, South Carolina and Mississippi — nine out of ten white persons disapproved of the ruling.

Recently another factor has entered the picture — namely, the amount of trouble which has occurred when efforts to integrate the schools have been made. Where there has been much trouble or violence, opposition to the Court decision has tended to stiffen; where integration has proceeded more or less smoothly (or where there has been no attempt to integrate), it has softened or in any event not increased.

Thus a repeat of the 1956 study — in late 1957 — found that there had been little change in the picture in the border states. It was in these states that most of the more peaceful integration attempts had been made. And in the Deep South, where practically no efforts to desegregate had been made, there was also little change — about nine out of ten whites in these states continued to oppose the Court decision.

In the Mid-South, however, resistance had definitely stiffened. In Arkansas, North Carolina and Virginia, trouble had broken out in one form or another in the period between the two surveys. In the earlier study, Mid-South opposition was about midway between the opposition in the border and Deep South states. By the end of 1957, white people in the Mid-South were lined up with those in their sister states of the old plantation South — with about nine out of ten now against the decision.

As trouble flared in one area after another, Southern whites displayed greater reluctance even to discuss the integration issue. A well-to-do Atlanta matron commented to a Gallup Poll reporter in late 1957: "It's just not something that the girls talk about over bridge anymore." If whites did not even want to talk about the question among themselves, it is even more obvious that any frank discussion of the issue between members of the two races was exceedingly difficult.

Southern whites and Negroes did report that they had

discussed desegregation with members of the opposite race. But when whites said they had discussed the issue with Negroes, the conversation they reported usually ran along the lines of one cited by a Georgia farm housewife:

"I've talked with the colored about this," she told a Gallup Poll reporter. "We talked about whether they'd be better off or worse in mixing. They don't want a change. The colored say please let them alone."

When Negroes said they had talked with whites, the conversation they reported was generally something like that mentioned by a North Carolina schoolteacher:

"These white people I talked with said they think integration can work. We talked about the way we thought it should happen."

What seemed to be happening, in short, was that both the white and colored South was hearing only what it wanted to hear about the race question in any interracial conversation.

As V. O. Key points out, "In its grand outlines the politics of the South revolves around the position of the Negro." Nothing has made this more meaningful than the political tides in the South since the Supreme Court decision — and particularly since Little Rock. The South is no longer just one-party, it is now one-policy so far as a candidate's stand on segregation is concerned. Taking any other than a stanch segregationist position is at present political suicide in most places in the South. The 1958 defeat of Arkansas's moderate Brooks Hays by the write-in segregationist Dale Alford was a clear-cut example.

The arrival of federal paratroopers in Little Rock may well have finished off the Republican party's chances in the South for the foreseeable future. And in the overwhelming Democratic dominance of the South lie many of the reasons for the GOP's present inability to achieve a Congressional majority. Because of the Solid South, the Democrats start every Congressional election campaign with a formidable advantage over the Republicans. The GOP needs to pile up a big majority in other areas of the country to offset this advantage — something they have been unable to do in recent elections.

Following the 1956 Presidential election, when Eisenhower polled a majority of the vote in the thirteen states of Dixie, the Republican outlook in that area was probably as bright as at any time since the Civil War. For the second successive election, the Eisenhower appeal to Southern voters had been strong enough really to disrupt traditional voting patterns. These two defections from the Democratic party were motivated primarily by an admiration for Eisenhower and not by such purely Southern factors as the 1948 Dixiecrat revolt over Truman's FEPC program or the 1928 vote for Herbert Hoover because of Al Smith's Catholicism and stand on Prohibition. The swing to Eisenhower in 1952 and 1956 was a positive kind of voter reaction; in 1928 and 1948 it had been a largely negative revolt *against* something.

When the Gallup Poll in early 1956 asked Southern whites what they felt the GOP could do in Dixie to build up a stronger party, the solution advanced most frequently was: "Get better candidates." The majority vote given

SOUTHERN REPUBLICANISM

Presidential Voting

	1928	1952	1956
Republican ticket	52	49	51
Democratic ticket	48	51	49

Eisenhower in November of that year was testimony that at least some Southern Democrats were serious about this suggestion. When the GOP had a candidate whom Southern voters liked (Eisenhower's popularity in the South, before Little Rock, often ran above the national level), they were not above voting for him.

Just ten months after Eisenhower got his Southern majority vote, however, he dispatched troopers of the 101st Airborne Division to Little Rock. When the Gallup Poll talked with Southern voters in the weeks following that action, there was widespread dissatisfaction with Eisenhower and the GOP for their handling of the situation. The general attitude can be summarized in the sentiment of one voter:

"Eisenhower said he wouldn't use force. He went back on his word."

When Southern whites were asked if their general attitude about the Republican party had changed in any way during the previous year, roughly three out of ten persons said it had. Virtually without exception, the change had been one for the worse for the GOP. Significantly the greatest change was noted among the Southern Democrats and Independents who had supported Eisenhower in 1956. A nurseryman from Chase City, Virginia, told one of our reporters: "The fact of the matter is I voted for Eisenhower last time. But now I'm going toward the Democrats again — I'm disappointed in Eisenhower."

LITTLE ROCK'S EFFECT ON GOP CHANCES

— Southern Eisenhower Voters — December, 1957 —

Southern:	Opinion of GOP in last year		
	Has Changed	*Has Not*	*Uncertain*
Republicans for Ike in 1956	20	74	6
Democrats for Ike in 1956	43	55	2
Independents for Ike in 1956	39	58	3

In many instances, of course, because the South is so heavily Democratic, the change was not so much a switch in allegiance as it was a further confirmation to a Southern Democrat that the Republicans were "no damn good." Typical was the wry comment of a young farm housewife who lived just outside of Clarksdale, Mississippi. She voted for Stevenson in 1956; she has yet in her life to vote Republican: "Oh yes, I've changed," she said, "I don't like the Republicans — only worse than I did before."

In the case of this housewife and many other dyed-in-the-wool Southern Democrats, the GOP did not lose a vote when federal troops moved into Little Rock. What they did lose, however, was the chance of these voters ever even considering a vote for the Republican party in the foreseeable future. And such a consideration had been entertained by about one Southern voter in three in a Gallup Poll in 1956 — or before Little Rock. In the November, 1956, elections, the GOP's share of the Congressional vote was higher than at any time since 1948. By 1958, the Republicans were back to their normal strength in the South — meaning a victory in about ten of the 120 seats at stake in that region and roughly 20 per cent of the total vote.

CONGRESSIONAL VOTE IN SOUTH — 1948-1958

	Democrats	Republicans
1948	79	21
1950	79.5	20.5
1952	80	20
1954	78	22
1956	73	27
1958	80	20

In various elections since the outbreak of racial turmoil in the South, the Democrats' task there has been made even easier than in the past. With most Southern elections decided in the primaries, the issue of who gets elected has often boiled down to the question of which candidate is the most outspoken segregationist. For the time being, a pro-segregation position is about the only one that any Southern candidate can take. Faced with a predominantly white electorate, overwhelmingly opposed to racial integration, there is little other choice. Until the whole racial question quiets down, this issue will continue to cloud the Southern political picture.

Which leads to a final question — when, if ever, *will* the racial issue quiet down? Is there a day in the future when the South will not be concerned about integration and segregation?

On several occasions since the 1954 decision, the Gallup Poll has asked Southern whites whether or not they believe integration — with white and colored going to the same schools, eating in the same restaurants and generally sharing facilities — will ever come to the South. Although the number who believe that integration will ultimately arrive has varied, it has always been larger than the number who feel this will never happen.

WILL INTEGRATION EVER COME TO SOUTH?

— Southern Whites —

	Yes	No	Uncertain
February, 1956	55	33	12
August, 1957	43	38	19
October, 1958	52	37	11

Eventual integration, however, is looked on as a bitter pill that the South will be forced to swallow because of "outside interests" and a North that "doesn't understand our problems." Almost two years before his city's name became a synonym for racial trouble, a Little Rock bus driver commented: "I think the North will cram it down our throats — and it will be sooner than you think."

A substantial minority of Southern whites, particularly

160

in the Deep South, refuses even to consider the question of *when* integration will come. The words of a Clarksdale, Mississippi, farmer in 1955 foreshadowed some of the school closings in the years that have followed:

"Well, maybe I'm just prejudiced," he said to one of our reporters. "I'm a Mississippi Southerner. But I think the people will continue to have separate schools indefinitely — if they have schools at all."

This farmer's view was even then in the minority — and events since 1955 have served to decrease the South's bitter-enders on segregation. Although the typical white Southerner sees much time and a good deal of trouble before integration comes, he feels that in the long run there is not much he can do to stop it — much as he might like to do so. One of the chief reasons why this is so results from the views held by the South's nearly ten million Negroes.

9

The Changing Negro South

ON THE OUTSKIRTS of a small Tennessee town not many miles from the battlefield at Shiloh, a group of unpainted shacks cluster just off the road leading out of town. In one of the shacks, the young Negro woman was asked about her politics. She shrugged and replied: "Huh! Neither Republican or Democrat. Here we're just colored folks."

Until recently, this would have served as an apt commentary on the status, both political and social, of most Southern Negroes. Since the 1954 Supreme Court decision, however, there have been clear indications that the Negro in the South is no longer willing to accept his social status with such resignation. And this dissatisfaction is reflected in his political outlook. The typical Southern Negro may still be neither Republican nor Democrat. In his convictions about what he wants, however, he has come some distance from being "just colored folks."

162

In the first year or two after the Supreme Court ruling, there was evidence that the Southern white's claim about Negroes not wanting integration was partially true. A special Gallup Poll study in early 1956 did turn up the fact that, a substantial number, if not a majority, of Southern Negroes did not then approve of the Court's ruling on desegregation in the schools.*

Negroes in the South obviously share a common desire to give their children the best possible education. This was true long before any Court ruling. But thoughts of integration with the South's vehemently anti-integration whites caused many a Negro to view with misgivings the possible repercussions when, and if, the time came to "mix in." Just the idea of such a radical departure — for both races — from an accepted Southern way of life left many Negroes honestly perplexed, confused, and wary of precipitate action.

THE CHANGING NEGRO SOUTH
Views on Supreme Court Decision

	Approve	Disapprove	No Opinion
February, 1956	53	36	11
December, 1957	69	13	18

*In its 1956 study of Southern Negro views, the Gallup Poll was in the process of training a staff of Negro reporters. Some of the Negroes were interviewed by Negroes, some by whites. Analysis showed little difference of opinion between those Negroes questioned by members of their own race and those interviewed by white reporters. In all subsequent studies, however, Southern Negroes were questioned only by Negro Group Poll interviewers. This permitted asking such questions as: "What things about your day-to-day dealings with white people bother you most?"

163

In the months that followed this 1956 study, racial disputes flared in many parts of the South. The Montgomery bus boycott, the Clinton riots, and, above all, the violence at Little Rock tended to confirm earlier views that "mixing in" would not be easy.

Yet a recheck on Southern Negro sentiment in the aftermath of Little Rock found a sharp increase in the proportion of Negroes who favored the Supreme Court decision. During this time, the percentage of Negroes who disapproved of the ruling had been cut to almost a third of what it had been in 1956.

CRUX OF THE SOUTH'S PROBLEM
Views on Court Decision — December, 1957

	Negro Views	White Views
Approve	69	15
Disapprove	13	83
No opinion	18	2

There seemed to be two major reasons for the increase in the Southern Negroes' support for integration. First, the Negro was inclined to feel that the integration dispute generally had helped rather than hurt him. The vote among those who expressed an opinion was 5 to 1 that it had helped. As a retired Alabama railroad worker put it, "I think it's helped us. It's sure given us more to look for in the future."

Second, the attacks on the Negro, both verbal and physical, during this period made Southern Negroes feel that it would be in a sense disloyal to their race if they were not to support the Supreme Court decision. This point was evidenced, for example, in the fact that in all segments of the Southern Negro population — young and old, college-trained as well as those with virtually no education, in cities and on farms in all parts of the South — substantial majorities approved of the decision.

SOUTHERN NEGRO VIEWS ON COURT RULING

— By Education — December, 1957

	Approve	Disapprove	No Opinion
College	89	3	8
High School	79	12	9
Grade or No School	66	14	20

The irony in the fact of the Negroes' unified position on integration is that such unanimity was caused chiefly by Southern white resistance. Before much trouble started, a substantial minority of Negroes opposed integration — something the whites wanted to believe. Because of the resistance of white segregationists, however, the Negroes unified to a point where denying them integration has become increasingly difficult. In this respect, white resistance has probably hastened the course of integration in the South.

This is obviously not to ignore the efforts of organizations such as the National Association for the Advancement of Colored People in trying to win support among Southern Negroes for integration. The Gallup Poll's 1957 study found that all but a few Southern Negroes were familiar with the NAACP. And the Negroes' opinion of

SOUTHERN NEGRO VIEWS OF NAACP

Heard of NAACP? — December, 1957 —

Yes	96
No	4

Opinion of NAACP? *

Favorable	69
Unfavorable	1
Undecided	30

*Asked of those familiar with organization

this organization was overwhelmingly favorable. But it seems unlikely that all of the pamphlets, talks and other educational efforts made by the NAACP could have had as much impact on Southern Negroes as did the headlines and TV and radio bulletins coming out of Montgomery, Clinton or Little Rock.

The Supreme Court school ruling became a symbol for the Negro — a way of expressing his general dissatisfaction with the way he was treated by the whites. Actually, the Southern Negro could think of a number of things which he found more irritating than the matter of segregated schools.

Gallup Poll reporters on this study (themselves Southern Negroes) asked Negroes what irritated them most in their day-to-day dealings with Southern whites. Only about one Negro in twenty-five said that his chief gripe was the segregated school system.

The chief irritant, in fact, had little or nothing to do with matters in which segregation or integration could be legislated. Most distasteful to Southern Negroes was the general attitude of the whites — the use of derogatory racial terms when referring to Negroes, and the assumption of superiority on the part of the Southern white.

Take, for example, the views of an Alabama schoolteacher, a graduate of one of that state's teachers colleges. What was it that made her most mad?

"To have them call me 'girl' when I am more than twice twenty-one," she said bitterly, "to have them use the word 'nigger' in my presence. To have them start to wait on me, then stop and wait on a white person."

The very argument that many whites use in defense of segregation — that many Negroes are "happier" with the way things are — is often a source of irritation. A Negro physician from Virginia put it this way:

"Most white people assume the idea that they know what the Negro wants and they assume the idea that they know what is good for the Negro. They make the sad mistake of portraying the idea that all Negroes are alike and if you see one or two you have the picture of the whole Negro race."

Here is a random selection of some further answers to the question of what irritates Negroes most in their dealings with whites:

"For them to refer to me as 'boy.'" "They figure all Negroes are children and don't believe we can think." "The way they talk to me . . ." "They refer to me as 'girl' or 'auntie' rather than as a lady." "They class me as not being human." "Lack of common courtesy . . ." "To refer to Negroes as 'niggers' . . ." "Saying 'boy' and 'girl' instead of Mr. and Mrs." "They don't honor me as a man."

167

It is only after irritants such as these that the Southern Negro mentions the things that have caused most of the trouble — sitting in the rear of the bus, being unable to sit down in restaurants, and segregated schools.

This is not to say that the Negro does not want to end segregation in the schools. When Gallup Poll reporters asked Southern Negroes specifically if they would prefer to keep their children in an all-Negro school, two out of three said they would not.

There is still a minority of Southern Negroes who disapprove of the Supreme Court's decision — about the same number, in fact, who would prefer to keep their children in an all-Negro school. Almost without exception, their reasons for feeling this way stem from a fear of the consequences of mixing the races in the schools. These Negroes are afraid of what might happen to their children if they went to school with white children; they wonder what kind of education they would get from white teachers. Typical of this viewpoint was the comment of a farm housewife from Cotton Plant, Arkansas:

"I think the colored children should stay in their own race," she said. "If all the children were to go to school together, I don't think they will get along. The white children will tramp on the colored children — and the colored children won't have a chance to learn like they should. I don't think the white teachers will take pains and teach the colored children."

As one means of bringing about integration, the Southern Negro has begun to focus attention on the voting booth. Although there are still few indications that he is actually using the vote as a weapon, there are a number of signs that he has become increasingly aware of just how potent his vote may be in the integration dispute.

Until fairly recently, the Southern Negro was disenfranchised throughout much of the South. And in many areas still, Negroes are kept from voting because of various types of pressures from the whites. In other areas of the South at present, where the Negro is able to vote, the tradition of *not* voting has been deeply ingrained. The total number of Negroes on voting rolls in the Southern states in 1958 — as estimated by the Southern Regional Council — was only 24 per cent of the Negroes of voting age in those states.*

NEGRO REGISTRATION vs. NEGRO POPULATION

	Per Cent Negro of Registration	Per Cent Negro of Population
Alabama	7	32
Arkansas	11	22
Florida	9	22
Georgia	12	31
Louisiana	14	33
Mississippi	7	45
North Carolina	8	27
South Carolina	11	39
Tennessee	13	16
Texas	7	13
Virginia	14	22

Source: 1958 Estimate by Southern Regional Council

*The Southern Regional Council's 1958 estimate did not include Kentucky or Oklahoma — two states which the Gallup Poll normally counts in the South. Since the proportion of Negroes in each of these states is relatively small (7% in Kentucky, 9% in Oklahoma), the 13-state picture of Negro voting would probably be about the same as the one referred to here.

169

The proportion of Negroes registered to vote in 1958, however, was considerably larger than it had been a decade earlier. The 24 per cent estimated as registered in 1958 was nearly twice the percentage registered in 1947.

The Gallup Poll's 1957 study among Southern Negroes found that this trend toward increased registration would likely continue unless the Negroes are further denied the vote. The weight of sentiment among Negroes interviewed was that more of their race would be registering to vote in future elections. Virtually no one thought Negro registrations would be slackening off. About six out of ten Southern Negroes who had never before voted said they planned to register to vote.

The chief reason why more Negroes were planning to vote was summed up in the bitterness of one Arkansas farmer who thought more members of his race in that state would be voting "to try to put our Governor out of office." In short, the Southern Negro tied increased voting directly to the integration issue. He was beginning to see some use to which his vote could be put. A young waitress from a Georgia farming community reasoned it this way:

"I just don't know how many will vote," she said, "but there'll be a lot of them. A lot were scared to vote, but

SOUTHERN NEGRO VOTING PLANS — 1957

Those Who Never Voted Say

Yes, I plan to register	57
No, no plans to register	14
Uncertain	29

170

they understand it more now that they've had it explained to them. They thought it was wrong before. Now they know."

Intention to register obviously is a far cry from an actual appearance at the polls on Election Day. But the important political fact is that the bulk of Southern Negroes in 1957 were at least giving some thought to the first step of registration.

The fact that more Southern Negroes were thinking about voting is just part of the picture. Of equal, if not greater, importance is *how* the newly registered Southern Negro may decide to vote and which of the two major parties he feels can do him the most good on the integration issue.

By tradition, the Southern Negro is a Republican — the first Republican President freed him from slavery; the GOP administrations that followed the Civil War encouraged the Negro's voting. In recent years, however, those few Negroes in the South who have voted have gone heavily Democratic — largely because of the influence of Franklin D. Roosevelt.

Eisenhower's decision to send federal troops to Little Rock met with widespread approval from Southern Negroes. But it was an approval accompanied by surprise — surprise that a Republican would take that much interest in the Negroes' cause. In addition, considering the bipartisan appeal of the President, it is extremely doubtful whether the Southern Negro attributed much partisan interest to the decision at Little Rock. He obviously liked Ike for what he did — there is little indication, however,

SOUTHERN NEGRO VIEW OF LITTLE ROCK

Opinions of Ike's Action in Sending Troops

Approve	78
Disapprove	7
No opinion	15

that he went a step farther and credited the GOP with this move.

The political outlook is clouded as far as Southern Negroes are concerned. Indications are that both the Republicans and the Democrats have fallen down in the matter of doing a real selling job with Negroes in the South. A majority of Southern Negroes (52 per cent) either said they didn't know which party Negroes should join or felt that there was no real difference between the two parties as far as Negroes were concerned. The great bulk of Southern Negroes were not united behind one party or the other.

Some idea of how Southern Negroes may react, if and when large numbers of them are voting, may be gained by a look at the voting behavior of Negroes in the North in recent years. On several occasions over the past few years the Gallup Poll has made special studies of the politics of the Northern Negro — seeking to measure both *how* and *why* he votes.

To Negroes everywhere in this country — whether in the Mississippi delta or the streets of Harlem — the name Roosevelt still has a much greater impact than that of Eisenhower.

Much of this impact, of course, can be attributed to the

late President's efforts in the field of civil rights. But more important, particularly when considering the Northern Negro's politics, is the fact that the party of Roosevelt is looked on as having given the Negro greater economic security than the party of Lincoln.

Nearly eight years of a Republican administration — during which several important steps in the civil rights field were taken — have done little to win the Northern Negro away from the Democratic party. The Negro in the North bases his politics as much on his pocketbook as he does on his race. And when he thinks of his pocketbook, he thinks Democratic.

NORTHERN NEGRO VOTE FOR CONGRESS

	Democratic	Republican
1954	77	23
1956	77	23
1958	72	28

Obviously, the Southern Negro's fight for integration has had tremendous impact among Northern Negroes. Emmett Till, Autherine Lucy, Martin Luther King and Daisy Bates are household words in New York's Harlem, Detroit's Paradise Valley, Chicago's South Side and other centers of Negro population in the Northern states. NAACP posters urging Negroes to "Join Now" are very much in evidence in shop windows and on walls in the Negro districts of Northern metropolitan areas. The Northern Negro has gone through much anguish over what he sees happening in some parts of the South.

173

But like most Americans, perhaps even more so than most, the Northern Negro's first concern is that of getting enough to feed, clothe and keep his family in decent fashion. The bitter refrain, "Last to be hired, first to be fired," is heard frequently from Negroes when they discuss their economic situation. Of necessity, the matter of finding a job and getting enough money to pay the bills takes on a greater personal importance than any political consideration of the civil rights dispute. And in this first, more personal concern, the memory of FDR's efforts to help the Negro bulks large.

And when the Northern Negro considers the civil rights dispute specifically, he is not ready to give the GOP much credit. Many Negroes, for example, think very highly of President Truman for his efforts with the Fair Employment Practices Commission. They have seen FEPC at work for some years; they have yet to see a great many Southern schools desegregate.

Because the Northern Negro regards the Democrats as his long-time friend in pocketbook matters, he feels that this friendship will carry over into the integration dispute. It is because of the economic security offered by the Democrats that he is able to stay with a party whose Southern wing numbers in its membership men like Mississippi's Senator James Eastland or Arkansas's Orval Faubus.

The Northern Negro is not happy about the Eastlands and the Faubuses being in the Democratic party. He seems to approach this dilemma, however, with a viewpoint of "out of sight, out of mind." When Negroes in the North talk about the Southern wing (and they rarely volunteer mention of this), they often seem to be thinking, in effect, about *two* Democratic parties. The one in the South may have its white supremacists. The other in the North has an Adam Clayton Powell in Harlem, a William Dawson in Chicago — and it had a Franklin D. Roosevelt.

The great majority of Northern Negroes will undoubtedly remain Democratic — the security they feel with this party is too deep-seated to permit any overnight switching because of recent Republican efforts on the civil rights front. And obviously the political views of the Northern Negro do filter through to the South. The Mason-Dixon line is no Iron Curtain. The voice of an Adam Clayton Powell is often heard as clearly in Montgomery as it is in Harlem.

The Southern Negro is just beginning to realize that there is power in his vote. For the time being, many Negroes in the South are content with the fact that they can vote — something they consider a giant step forward. Once they are certain that this privilege will not be taken away from them — and many, for obvious reasons, are not yet certain of this — they will no doubt do much serious thinking about just how to use it to their best advantage.

If the Southern Negroes should move into the Republican party's ranks in wholesale fashion, such a move would probably reinforce long-term Southern white views that

175

the GOP is the "Negro party." In most places in the South, the Negro Republicans would be heavily outvoted on Election Day by the white Democrats.

If, on the other hand, Negroes in the Southern states should swing en masse into the Democratic party, their bloc voting could have some interesting repercussions on the South's primary system. The victor in many Southern Democratic primaries often has only a small plurality of the votes. Suppose, for example, that one candidate out of a field of five or six *deliberately* appealed to Negro voters on a moderate platform — and won by virtue of Negro bloc voting. Granted that the ensuing run-off primary — held in most Southern states when no candidate receives a majority of the vote in the first primary — would probably produce mass white voting as a counter-action. Yet there is a minority of Southern whites who approve of the Supreme Court decision and who might also be drawn to the moderate candidate. And the very implication that a candidate might aid his cause by appealing to Negro voters would probably send shock waves reverberating down the political corridors of the South. It would offer some other platform to a candidate than the only one he can choose now of trying to out-segregation his opponent. The Southern Negro vote, now only a minor force in the politics of that region, might in time to come be something to reckon with in the Southern electorate.

10

Lame Ducks Finish Strong

AT A PRESS CONFERENCE near the beginning of Eisenhower's last year in office, one reporter asked a question
in which it appeared to Mr. Eisenhower that he was being
charged with partisanship in his management of our
military defenses. The President was obviously irked by
the question. He reddened and, in starting to answer,
snapped back, "First of all, I don't *have* to be partisan!"

Eisenhower was the first Chief Executive in forty years,
if not the first in our history, who could make such a
statement. Woodrow Wilson was the last President to
have served the traditional limit of two terms. Roosevelt,
in 1940, shattered the tradition of no third term. Truman,
in 1952, was still legally able to seek re-election if he
chose to do so. Eisenhower was the first to be constitu-
tionally barred from running again. As he stated em-
phatically to the reporter, during the Lame Duck stage of
his administration, he did not "have to be partisan." In

this fact lies much of the explanation for Ike's strength with the American public during the closing years of his Presidency.

When Eisenhower started his second term in 1957, there was much political prophecy about the loss of power the President would suffer because of the restriction imposed by the Twenty-second Amendment. Eisenhower would be unable to hold his own party in line, many reasoned, and he stood to lose much of the respect he then commanded from the American voter.

During the first half of Ike's second term, it appeared as if the prophets might have been right — at least as to the American public's reaction. It was not until after the 1958 Congressional election, when the President's obligation to sell the Republican party had been fulfilled, that the full impact of the second-term limitation became evident. By the end of 1959, the President — just returned from a triumphal tour of eleven nations — had recouped much of the popularity loss of the first half of his second term. He received a vote of confidence from the American public which was higher than any recorded by the Gallup Poll since the early months of 1957. During the first few months of 1960, Eisenhower's popularity slipped off somewhat, but he continued to get an approval vote from a substantial majority of voters. With partisan interest reawakened by the coming elections, most of his loss came in the Democratic ranks.

In his book *Presidential Power,* Richard Neustadt offers this suggestion about the source of a Chief Executive's strength with the electorate: "An image of the office, not an image of the man, is the dynamic factor in a President's prestige. Impressions of the person will form early and last long, but the values men assign to what they can see alter rather quickly."

What the American voters thought they could *see* throughout 1959 was a Presidency in which there were obviously no more worries about re-election. Eisenhower's actions appeared to be free of partisan motives. The *office* had changed — the White House was no longer a branch of Republican party headquarters; its function was now, purely and simply, to look out for the interests of all Americans regardless of party.

Admittedly this is oversimplification of the situation. Eisenhower *is* a Republican; he would like to see a Republican take over the White House and he is doing what he can to see that this happens. But Eisenhower *personally* is not seeking re-election. And oversimplication is sometimes helpful in understanding those basic, often vaguely defined currents of public opinion which have at times altered the American political picture. This is true if only because voters themselves sometimes oversimplify the issue.

If such a change in the voters' image of the office was occurring in 1959, the fact that it happened with Eisenhower — whose strength has always stemmed from his bipartisan appeal — only served to speed the process. It is noteworthy, incidentally, that Truman's popularity went up in 1952 after he announced he would not seek re-election.

The upswing in Eisenhower's popularity following the

1958 Congressional elections is all the more dramatic when contrasted with the first two years of his second term. When the Eisenhower record is all in, the years 1957 and 1958 will probably stand out as the President's doldrum years. Eisenhower's popularity with the public slipped badly, and the Republican administration suffered a series of setbacks on both domestic and international fronts.

In January, 1957, Eisenhower's popularity with the public equaled his first-term high point of 79 per cent, after the 1955 Geneva summit conference. By the middle of 1957, it had slipped off some 17 percentage points — the sharpest decline in his popularity during a comparable period recorded by the Gallup Poll. By the end of 1957, it was back down to the low point of his first term — 57 per cent.

Mr. Eisenhower was apparently not the only American with worries in 1957. A Gallup Poll that spring found that an estimated seven million Americans had already tried one of the new tranquilizer pills. Reactions on the Road to Miltown were varied — a midtown Manhattan actress told a Gallup Poll reporter that the pills made her more depressed, a farm housewife from Beaver Dam, Kentucky (population 1349), who felt that "we are living too fast and we need something to tone it down," reported that her happy pills "gave me a kind of relaxed feeling." In Minneapolis, a sleepy-eyed user of tranquilizers yawned her reaction to our reporter: "They sure do the job." For what it's worth, a breakdown found that proportionately more Republicans than Democrats had taken a tranquilizer.

The first half of 1957 was highlighted by two domestic battles. The first was over the President's budget; the second, triggered by the first, was a new round in the fight between "Eisenhower" Republicans and "Taft" Republicans. From both of these struggles Ike emerged as the eventual loser in the court of public opinion.

EISENHOWER'S DOLDRUM YEARS — 1957-1958
Percentage Approving President's Performance in Office

January, 1957	79
March	72
June	62
November	57
January, 1958	60
March	52
April	49
May	54
August	58
November	52

When Eisenhower fought to defend his record peacetime budget for 1957 of nearly 72 billion dollars, he took a stand which was unpopular with voters. In addition, the budget was of course complicated to get across to the public. Gallup Polls have shown that even the basic mechanics of the federal government's economics are matters which the average American has a difficult time comprehending. Throughout the late winter and spring of 1957, polls consistently found the weight of public opinion siding with the critics who favored a budget cut.

181

In singling out foreign aid as the one area of the budget for which he decided to fight more strongly, Eisenhower selected a particularly unpopular cause. Those relatively few voters who understood some of the details of our mutual security program tended to support it. But the great majority of American voters in the spring of 1957 could not tell you much about foreign aid — they only knew they were against it. (Americans are not necessarily at a loss for an opinion just because of lack of knowledge. Another poll that spring found that four out of ten people didn't know where the Kremlin was; this didn't prevent them from being anti-Communist.)

Eisenhower had the cards stacked against him when he went to the people in late May of 1957 to appeal for support for his foreign aid program. A Gallup Poll check on his two national TV-radio speeches showed some shift in sentiment to the President's side, but opinion continued to favor a cut in the mutual security program.

Many of Eisenhower's opponents in the budget fight came from within his own party. (One even came from within his own family — his brother Edgar was quoted as saying that he would "sure like to discover what influence is at work on my brother.") Discontent among the so-called "Taft" Republicans served to renew the argument of some year's standing between the conservative and liberal wings of the Republican party.

When the public was informed of some of the basic differences between Taft and Eisenhower Republicanism, and asked to choose between the two, the latter brand won hands down. But if the President won the battle here, he

TWO KINDS OF REPUBLICANISM
March, 1957

All Voters

Prefer Eisenhower Republicans	74
Prefer Taft Republicans	18
No opinion	8

perhaps lost the war — a war in which he personally never took a position of clear and strong leadership. Ike's popularity has always been sensitive to exactly this kind of indecision which seemed to voters to personify his role in the battle betwen the two wings of the GOP. In taking a strong stand for *his* brand of Republicanism, Eisenhower might possibly have made some sorely needed converts to the GOP, even if, in so doing, he lost the support of some right-wing GOP voters.

As it was, the President lost the support of some conservative Republican voters. His popularity among Presidential supporters of Senate Minority Leader William F. Knowland—acknowledged right-wing leader—was about

TWO KINDS OF REPUBLICANISM
June, 1957

	Eisenhower's Popularity Among	
	Nixon Supporters	*Knowland Supporters*
Approve	83	51
Disapprove	9	30
No opinion	8	19

ten points below what it was nationally in the middle of 1957. Among those Republicans who favored the nomination of Vice-President Nixon — the spokesman for Eisenhower Republicanism — Ike's popularity was considerably above the national average of 62 per cent.

Eisenhower might be able to afford a loss in voter popularity. His party could not. The GOP had been unable to regain control of Congress in 1956. As Eisenhower's standing with voters dropped, the Republican party's strength plummeted to a point where a Gallup Poll roundup carried the summary question: "Is the GOP Headed for the Rocks?"

By the summer of 1957, the best the Republicans could do outside the South was an even split in the Gallup Poll's measure of the Congressional vote. Normally they should poll about 55 per cent of the Congressional vote in the Northern and Western states if they hope to offset the Democrats' Southern advantage. In the South, GOP strength had again slipped back after the slight increase in their vote at the time of Eisenhower's 1956 victory — they had their normal Southern quota of about one vote in five.

The Democratic trend spread far and wide. Defections from the GOP ranks were noted in the heavily industrial East and in the rural Midwest, the latter traditionally the heartland of Republicanism.

The GOP was not getting across to voters the idea that the Republican party had the voters' self-interest at heart. In the bulk of the electorate — the skilled and unskilled workers and their families, the farming people of the nation — the Democrats had the advantage in the matter of which party looked out for their interests best. The

WHICH PARTY SERVES YOUR INTERESTS BEST?
June, 1957

	Business & Professional	White-collar	Farmers	Skilled Workers	Unskilled Workers
Republican	53	43	22	22	15
Democratic	25	25	48	48	50
No difference, No opinion	22	32	30	30	35

Republicans were ahead with only two groups — the business and professional people and the white-collar workers. When a Gallup Poll re-registered the total electorate in the summer of 1957 — by asking how voters would sign up if forced to register anew — the Democrats had an estimated edge of nearly 13 million potential voters.

IF ALL VOTERS REGISTERED AGAIN — 1957*
Would Sign Up as

Democrats	51,600,000
Republicans	39,000,000
On the Fence	8,600,000

*Based on estimated 99.2 million civilian citizens of voting age.

Events in the fall of 1957 only compounded the President's difficulties as first Little Rock, then Sputnik made headlines around the world.

Although Eisenhower won support in the North for his decision to send troops into Little Rock, his action infuriated many white Southerners. Eisenhower's popularity in the South had often been above that recorded nationwide. Since Little Rock, his Southern popularity

IKE'S SENDING TROOPS TO LITTLE ROCK?
September, 1957

| | Opinions of | |
	Northerners	Southerners
Right thing	74	36
Wrong thing	16	53
Undecided	10	11

has been below the national average. Two years after the arrival of paratroopers in Arkansas, Gallup Poll reporters often encountered Southern voters whose sole reason for disapproving of Eisenhower was "because he sent the Army to Little Rock."

While hardly recovered from the racial crisis, American public opinion was confronted with an even more frightening issue — the race for space. By late November, a Gallup Poll estimated that some four million Americans had seen either Sputnik I or II with their own eyes. About the same number of Americans, coincidentally, were ready to volunteer to be the first man or woman in space when, and if, the United States was prepared to take this step.

The public's surprise at the Sputniks turned to shock and then, in many instances, to downright anger. By a 5-to-3 vote the American people said they believed this meant the Soviets were ahead of us in military power. And the public could see few reasons for their getting ahead of us other than the simple fact that the Soviets had worked harder and spent more money. Americans had been willing to spend more for some years — by a curious coincidence, a Gallup Poll released just ten years to the day before the first Sputnik was launched reported the public in favor of this country's alloting more funds to scientific research in order to keep up with Russia.

A previously nonexistent problem — that of keeping up with the Russians in the space race — jumped into fourth place as one of the major issues facing the country. In another Gallup Poll, the public believed it was time for the United States to take a new look at our defense policies. When asked who or what was at fault for our lagging behind Russia, the public placed the blame squarely in the lap of the Eisenhower administration.

At year's end the President's popularity was down to his first-term low point of 57 per cent. And ahead lay a situation where the GOP would be particularly vulnerable — the 1958 recession. If there is one damaging image which the Republican party has been unable to drive from voters' minds, it is that they are the depression party, chiefly to blame for the economic slump of the 1930s. Despite the general prosperity of the Eisenhower years, this is one recurring theme when voters are asked what the Republican party means to them.

The 1958 slump did not of course approach the depression of the 1930s. At the peak of unemployment in April, the number out of work was considerably lower than in 1937. Less than half of the people interviewed by the Gallup Poll in early April, 1958, said they had been affected by the recession in any way. And the public thought of the situation as only a recession, not a depression. By way of further comparison, the 1937 condition was definitely considered a *depression* in a Gallup Poll at the time.

187

In the very middle of the recession, there was time for less bothersome issues. Time, for example, to vote overwhelming against the new sack dress — 86 in every 100 said they didn't like this style. One man's comment was typical of the sentiment of many — "I've seen potatoes in better ones." And there was time to establish for posterity that Americans in April, 1958, believed middle age started when you were forty-two and a half years old and that a woman reached the peak of her beauty at thirty.

The very words recession and depression, however, were enough to scare voters away from the Republican party. For the first time since 1937, a Gallup Poll in March found unemployment topping the list of what voters considered to be the most important problems facing the country. For the first time Eisenhower's popularity dipped below the 50 per cent line (to 49). The GOP strength nationwide was nearly as low as it had been in 1936. A majority of Republican voters in May, 1958, had already conceded the coming November elections.

The public still admired Ike as a person. When people were asked by the Gallup Poll to invite any three persons from all history to their house for dinner, Eisenhower, along with Lincoln and FDR, got the most invitations. There were some slightly more off-beat combinations. One woman thought an interesting dinner party would be made up of Socrates, Diogenes and Jack Paar. A man said his choice would be Lincoln, Will Rogers and Marilyn Monroe. Another man would invite FDR, Alexander Hamilton and Pancho Villa. Nearly four hundred famous personages in all received dinner invitations in this Gallup Poll.

From the spring of 1958 until the actual voting, there was little real change in the size of the Republican vote measured by successive Gallup Polls. When the results were all in, Democratic contenders in the House races had piled up a Democratic majority bigger than any since 1936. The last few weeks of the campaign saw a slight swing to the GOP, sparked by last-minute campaign efforts of Eisenhower and Nixon, but it was too late to make much difference. The Democrats were in with a whopping 130-seat margin in the House and a control of the Senate so overwhelming that it ruled out Republican hopes of winning the upper chamber in 1960.

The downward trend of Eisenhower's personal popularity throughout 1958 was interrupted twice. In May it showed a sharp upswing following the President's spirited defense of his Pentagon reorganization plan — from the April low point of 49 to 54 per cent. Three months later, Eisenhower's dispatch of United States Marines to Lebanon proved another shot in the arm to his popularity — from 52 to 58 per cent. When asked specifically about the decision to send troops to the revolt-torn Near Eastern country, 54 per cent of the public approved, only 27 per cent disapproved.

The Sherman Adams case broke that summer and caused much speculation that it would severely damage the President's prestige. Actually, it had no sharp impact on Eisenhower's popularity. Adams's name, in fact, had come up occasionally when voters criticized the men *around* Eisenhower, but not the President himself. Some seven out of ten Americans in July said they were familiar with the case of Adams taking gifts from industrialist Bernard Goldfine. Among those who were following the case, the weight of sentiment was that Adams should resign. When the public was asked, however, if there were more or less dishonesty under Eisenhower than under Truman, most people said they guessed things were about the same. Among those who did see a difference, the GOP administration got a slightly higher honesty rating. And Eisenhower's popularity showed little change in polls taken before and after the incident.

After the Lebanese incident, the President's popularity once again fell off. By the time of the November Congregational voting, it was hovering just above the 50 per cent line. Considering most other political indicators at the time, the evidence suggested that Eisenhower's rating with voters would either level off at about this point or continue to fall even lower. More than ever, Ike was now a lame duck President — and he faced a near-record majority of Democrats in the new Congress. Many of them were liberals and Eisenhower was clearly determined to fight this majority on the issue of government spending and inflation — an issue which had fallen flat in the President's pre-election campaigning. It was not a situation where an increase in Eisenhower's personal popularity seemed indicated. Yet in just a few months exactly that was happening.

The sense of paradox is heightened by the fact that the

190

Republican party's strength, measured in Gallup Polls on the Congressional races, continued to fall below the already low level of the 1958 elections. By May of 1959, GOP strength was down to its lowest point in the twentieth century — if not, in fact, the lowest point in the whole history of the Grand Old Party.

Throughout the first half of 1959, Eisenhower's rising popularity continued as an amazing and seemingly inexplicable phenomenon. Only two months after the 1958 elections, he had regained much of the support he had lost during the entire past twelve months. By midsummer, his popularity was as high as any recorded by the Gallup Poll in almost two years. By the end of 1959, some seven out of ten voters across the country approved of the way he was handling the Presidency.

Obviously, Eisenhower's decision in the summer to invite Nikita Khrushchev to the United States and to accept an invitation to visit the Soviet Union himself helped the President's popularity during the latter half of the year. It was exactly the kind of decisiveness which voters liked

EISENHOWER COMES BACK — 1959

Percentage Approving His Performance

November, 1958	52
January, 1959	57
March	59
May	61
July	63
September	64
November	66
December	71

191

to see in Ike. Khrushchev's visit here in the fall was widely approved in Gallup Polls taken both before and after the tour. And the new heights in Eisenhower's popularity near the end of 1959 were ample testimony to how much the public approved of the President's good will tour to Asian, European and African nations.

Before any of these developments on the international scene, however, Ike's popularity had been on the rise for eight or nine months. By the time political observers began to talk about the "new Eisenhower" in the early summer, the President had been, if not the new certainly the better-liked Eisenhower for several months.

There are few indications of anything specific which the President said or did in early 1959 to explain this rise in popularity. The fight against inflation, for example, seemed to be profiting the Democrats more than the Republicans. Any mention of inflation seemed to serve

WHICH PARTY CAN HANDLE HIGH PRICES BETTER?

	June, 1959	September, 1959
Democrats	38	39
Republicans	23	25
No difference, No opinion	39	36

chiefly as a reminder to voters that prices were high. And on two occasions in 1959, voters picked the Democrats over the Republicans as the party which they felt could do the better job of handling high prices. The administration was just not getting the electorate to make the connection between the GOP's stated concern with inflation and higher prices. And there is little to indicate that Ike's concern with this problem helped him specifically with the public.

At least part of the explanation for Eisenhower's increased popularity during early 1959 may be in the simple fact of his not being able to seek re-election. A full two years before the end of his Presidency, he could assume the elder statesman role normally assigned to former Chief Executives. This was the change in the public's image of the *office* of the Presidency.

Helping to propel this change was the fact that things seemed to voters to be running pretty smoothly between the Republican White House and the Democratic Capitol Hill. There were obviously disputes, but few of the pyrotechnics which had seemed likely between Democratic liberals and the anti-spending Eisenhower. In the summer of 1959, voters in a Gallup Poll were by no means dissatisfied with the divided government in Washington — more said it was a good than a bad thing.

When Eisenhower — the new kind of lame duck — decided to make a personal try at easing world tensions, his action boosted his popularity that much higher. If the peoples of Europe welcomed Eisenhower with fond remembrances of his World War II performances, the American people sent him abroad with much the same remembrances in their minds. This was the Eisenhower the public had admired so greatly and wanted so badly for years before he was first elected.

193

11

The Catholic Vote -- Chicken or Egg?

FEW PEOPLE would have blamed Senator John Kennedy
if he were slightly out of sorts on a morning in late November of 1959. As a leading contender for the 1960
Democratic nomination, and a Roman Catholic, Kennedy
could hardly have welcomed any stirring up of religious
controversy in the electorate. Yet a front-page story that
day had just tossed into the political arena one of the
touchiest of all Protestant-Catholic controversies — birth
control. A statement strongly condemning any official
United States attempt to supply birth control information
to other nations had just been issued by the American
Catholic hierarchy.

The ensuing storm over the birth control question
served to confirm one obvious, if distasteful, fact about
American politics. Namely, that with a Roman Catholic
involved in Presidential speculation, the religious issue
was bound to be a consideration. Kennedy's appeal to

Wisconsin Catholics in the 1960 primary seemed a surprise to some political observers — it shouldn't have been.

The specific controversy over the birth control issue did not seem to be of great concern at the grass roots level. Three out of four Americans said they had heard about the world's predicted population explosion, but only one in five was worried about it. A majority of the public did believe that if a country asked for birth control information, the United Nations should supply it to them; an even larger majority thought that people in this country who wanted such information should be able to get it. But this was motivated by a desire to be democratic about the whole thing more than it was a worry over too many babies. There was at that time, in fact, an increased number of Americans who felt that large families (four or more children) were a good thing.

If there was any political effect from the birth control controversy, it was probably an indirect one which helped Kennedy more than it hurt him. The publicity about the Massachusetts Senator's stand on the issue certainly made more people aware that Kennedy was a Catholic. And with primary races facing him in New Hampshire and Wisconsin — both states with large numbers of Catholic voters — this awareness was a plus factor for Kennedy.

One of the most amazing findings the Gallup Poll ever turned up was that in the spring of 1959 over half (53 per cent) of all Americans did not know that Kennedy was a Catholic. About four Catholic voters in ten did not know the Senator's religion. By early in 1960, over eight out of ten Catholic voters knew that Kennedy was

HOW MANY KNOW KENNEDY IS CATHOLIC?

Aware of Senator's Religion

	May, 1959	March, 1960
All voters	47	69
Protestants	42	64
Catholics	61	82

a Catholic; overall, the awareness of Kennedy's religion had gone from 47 to 69 per cent. During the fall of 1959 and early 1960, Kennedy was gaining ground on Vice-President Nixon among the nation's Catholic voters in Gallup Poll tests. Certainly one factor here was the increasing number of Catholics who came to know that Kennedy was a Catholic.

KENNEDY GAINS AMONG CATHOLICS

Percentage of Catholics voting for Kennedy when opposing Nixon

	September, 1959	January, 1960
All Catholics	63	72
Catholic Democrats	80	88
Catholic Republicans	22	27
Catholic Independents	64	62

Invariably, a Catholic candidate's attraction for his fellow Catholics may trigger a Protestant reaction. But it ought to be pointed out in Kennedy's case that a majority of Catholics would probably vote Democratic anyway and that a majority of Protestants outside of the South normally vote Republican. These lines have been drawn chiefly for economic and not religious reasons. Many Catholics tend to come from the lower end of the economic scale and are thus drawn to the Democratic party; many Protestants are in the upper economic groups and have gravitated to the GOP.

In attempting to explain the religious issue in voting, one quickly runs into the old question of which came first, the chicken or the egg. Are Catholics drawn to Kennedy partly through a natural resentment over there never having been a Catholic President? In turn, just how much Protestant counter-reaction is due to a natural concern over Catholics ganging up behind a Catholic candidate?

Surveys indicate that the great majority of Americans have no objection to voting for a Catholic for President. In Gallup Polls since 1937, majorities have consistently endorsed the principle that a man's religious beliefs should be no bar to the Presidency. Prejudice against a Catholic for President has been declining over the last twenty years. And the public's open-mindedness is not reserved for a Catholic candidate alone. A 1958 Gallup Poll found substantial majorities who said they would vote for either a Catholic or a Jew if he were their party's Presidential nominee. The one thing that the public would require, apparently, is that a candidate have *some* religion —

RELIGION A BAR TO THE PRESIDENCY?
October, 1958

| | How Voters Feel About Supporting | | |
	Catholic	Jew	Atheist
Would vote for him	68	62	18
Would not	25	28	75
Don't know	7	10	7

three out of four Americans in the same poll said they would *not* vote for their party's candidate if he were an atheist.

Any Catholic Presidential nominee, however, would have to face the fact that a minority of the electorate would feel that his religion was sufficient to bar him from the White House. The size of this group (about one person in four) would mean a considerable proportion of the vote that a Catholic would have to spot his opponent before the race even got under way.

There are a number of questions which non-Catholics might logically be expected to raise over a Catholic's candidacy — his stand on supplying birth control information or state aid to parochial schools or sending an ambassador to the Vatican. A Catholic President could conceivably be forced to make decisions on these issues; they are things which have concerned a number of leading Protestant clergy and laymen.

But these specific items are rarely mentioned by voters who object to a Catholic for President. Anti-Catholicism more often involves a fear of something highly unlikely ("The Pope would come over here and run the White House") or it comes from an almost instinctive mistrust of something with which voters are unfamiliar. In a number of instances, voters say in effect that they don't know just what it is that Catholics believe in, but that they are certain it is alien to their own personal religious beliefs. This mistrust is often vaguely defined; voters offer such reasons as "Because I'm not a Catholic," or "Because I don't believe in that religion."

In at least a few instances, opposition to a Catholic is obviously based on misinformation about the United States political system or the Catholic religion itself. A Maryland woman, for example, would not vote for a Catholic "because it's not according to the Constitution." A Virginia man didn't want a Catholic because "they don't believe in the Virgin Mary and the Holy Ghost like we do."

Protestant objection to a Catholic President is centered most heavily in the region where there have always been the fewest Catholics — the South. The least degree of Protestant opposition is found in New England where Catholic populations are the heaviest.

Many of the reasons why some voters would not like to see a Catholic President have probably changed little over the years. The cry "Rum, Romanism and Rebellion" would no doubt still strike a responsive chord in some areas today. Many of the prejudices today are the same as those which Al Smith had to contend with in 1928.

There were other factors than anti-Catholicism involved in the South's defection in 1928. The man whose manner of speech obviously came straight from the sidewalks of New York was not exactly the type a rural Southerner would warm to. And Al Smith's advocacy of the repeal of Prohibition certainly offended some dry voters from the Bible Belt. Key's analysis of the 1928 election shows that defections from the Democratic ticket were most marked in those counties where there were the fewest Negroes, least noticeable in the "black-belt" counties where the proportion of Negroes was heaviest. This same

199

IN YOUR OPINION

THE SOUTH BOLTS TO HOOVER
— *1928 Election* —
Major Party Voting

	Hoover	Smith
Total South	52.0	48.0
"Hoover" states:		
Oklahoma	64.3	35.7
Kentucky	59.4	40.6
Florida	58.6	41.4
Tennessee	55.4	44.6
North Carolina	54.9	45.1
Virginia	54.0	46.0
Texas	52.0	48.0
"Smith" states:		
Alabama	48.6	51.4
Georgia	44.0	56.0
Arkansas	39.5	60.5
Louisiana	23.7	76.3
Mississippi	17.4	82.6
South Carolina	4.8	95.2

division has also often marked the difference between the dry vote in the upland hill country of the small farmer and the wet vote of the planter down along the delta. But Smith's religion was also a large factor. If anything, his Northern big-city background plus his opposition to Prohibition helped to complete many Southerners' image of the Roman Catholic as a minority-group immigrant from Northern tenements who liked to drink.

The South remains the center of opposition to a Catholic President. About one voter in three in these thirteen states in 1959 indicated that he would not vote for his party's candidate if he were a Catholic; another one in eight was uncertain. Analysis indicates that most of the No Opinion voters swing into a position of opposing a Catholic when forced into stating an opinion one way or the other. It is not exactly a completely neutral uncertainty — more a case of having some misgivings about voting for a Catholic. Thus there may be little apparent

SOUTHERN MISGIVINGS
Vote for a Catholic?

	1959	1940
Yes, definitely would	53	51
No, or some misgivings	47	49

change on the religious issue in the South over the last two decades. As in a 1940 Gallup Poll, nearly half of the persons questioned today have at least some misgivings about voting for a Catholic.

Anti-Catholic sentiment at present is much more marked in the states of the Mid-South — Arkansas, Florida, North Carolina and Virginia — than it is in the Deep South states of Alabama, Georgia, Louisiana, Mississippi and South Carolina. And it was the Mid-South much more than the Deep South which went so heavily against Smith. With the exception of Arkansas, home state of the Democratic Vice-Presidential candidate, Joseph T. Robinson, all of the normally Democratic Mid-South states went heavily Republican in 1928. The Deep South states remained in the Democratic column.* This parallel between the 1928 vote and the degree of anti-Catholicism at present seems to reinforce the argument that Smith's poor Southern showing was due in a large measure to his religion.

The generally low voting turnout in this region, however, may tend to lessen the total impact of the South's resistance on this question. With an extremely low proportion of Negroes voting, plus a general apathy at election time because of one-party dominance, the percentage of voters who get to the polls in the South is usually far below the national average. Over the last twenty years, the rate of turnout in the South in Presidential elections has averaged about half the turnout rate in other regions of the country.

Just how much effect the religious issue could have on turnout is extremely difficult to judge. A great many more Americans voted in 1928 than in 1924, but this was probably due as much to the increasing number of women voters as it was anything else. The higher turnout was no more marked in the South than elsewhere.

On a national basis, the opposition to a Catholic candidate is higher among voters with only grade school education than among voters with high school and college

*In analyzing the 1928 vote, V. O. Key notes the tendency of white voters in heavily Negro areas to stay with the Democrats and says this was due to their anxiety over racial problems. Elsewhere the whites "could afford the luxury of voting their convictions on the religious and prohibition issues." Today, however, the Mid-South has *both* anti-Catholicism and racial anxiety — some of the most serious desegregation disputes have come in the Mid-South states. Could the Mid-South today still "afford the luxury" of voting on religious issues, or would they prefer a Catholic Democrat to a Republican Protestant like Nixon who has been closely identified with the civil rights fight?

education. And generally speaking, the lower down the educational scale a voter stands, the lower is his interest in voting. In short, much of the anti-Catholic sentiment comes from people who may not turn up at the polls on Election Day.

VOTE FOR A CATHOLIC?
By Education Levels

	College Voters	High School Voters	Grade School Voters
Would vote for him	74	71	58
Would not	22	23	31
Don't know	4	6	11

The returns from the 1960 Wisconsin primary made it clear that Senator Kennedy had a great appeal to the Catholics; a number of Catholic Republicans had crossed over to vote for Kennedy in the Democratic primary. This same pattern seems to hold true at the national level among Catholic voters interviewed by the Gallup Poll. Although some official circles in the Catholic church have expressed concern over this trend,* a good number of America's Catholics are apparently prepared to vote for a Catholic regardless of his party. A Gallup Poll in the spring of 1959 found that Senator Kennedy might be helped considerably by votes from Catholic Republicans.

About one voter in four who cast a ballot in the 1956 Presidential election was a Roman Catholic. And there is

*For example, in an editorial in April, 1960, *The Monitor,* newspaper of the Trenton, N.J., diocese, stated that Catholics might be guilty of grave sin if they voted for a Catholic nominee purely on a religious basis.

considerable talk among Catholics about the fact that only once has a Catholic ever been nominated for the Presidency. When questioning Catholic voters about the issue, Gallup Poll reporters often hear comments such as "We've never had a Catholic President — I think it would be good if we had one," or "I don't see why a Catholic shouldn't have as much chance as anyone else." The inevitable effect of sentiment like this is the appeal that a Catholic candidate has to some Catholic voters, no matter what his or their political views.

RELIGION OF UNITED STATES VOTERS
—1959 —

Protestant	66
Roman Catholic	26
Jewish	4
Other or None	4

— Based on Gallup Poll data

A party with a Catholic candidate heading the ticket could normally count on overwhelming support from Catholic voters within the party rank and file. All but a negligible few Catholics — who chiefly fear possible increase in religious bigotry — say they would support a Catholic candidate of their party in a Presidential election.

VOTE FOR A CATHOLIC FROM YOUR PARTY?
— Catholics Only —

Would vote for him	95
Would not	2
Don't know	3

A truer measure of how strongly Catholics feel about this religious issue is the question of how many Catholics might bolt their party if the rival party nominated a Catholic for President. A 1959 Gallup Poll indicated that perhaps half of all Catholics *might* bolt under these circumstances. Less than four Catholics in ten said they definitely would *not* leave the party of their choice to vote for the Catholic candidate. It should be emphasized

HOW MANY CATHOLICS MIGHT BOLT TO RIVAL
TICKET'S CATHOLIC CANDIDATE?

Yes, might bolt	52
No, would not	37
Don't know	11

that the question asked only if they would think about making such a move, not whether they would actually do so. Comments from Catholic voters indicate that many would make such a switch only "if I thought he was a good man." But the findings do give some idea of the possible repercussions which the candidacy of a Roman Catholic might have in the opposition party's camp.

This kind of Catholic attitude is no respecter of party lines — Catholic Republicans and Catholic Democrats give approximately the same response to these questions. In trying to interpret just what this might mean in a Presidential race, however, one is confronted with a sort of political chessboard on which it is necessary to consider (1) the line-ups of the parties in this country, and (2) the distribution of Catholics within the ranks of each party.

RELIGION IN UNITED STATES POLITICS — 1959

Religious Affiliation

	All Voters	Republican Voters	Democratic Voters	Independent Voters
Protestant	66	78	62	60
Catholic	26	16	31	27
Other, None	8	6	7	13

For the Democrats, a Catholic nominee would mean that they would hold most of their own Catholic voters. This constitutes a sizable proportion of the Democratic party whose defections in the past have often proved disastrous. In addition, they might pick up about half of all Republican Catholics — or about one GOP voter in fourteen.

If the Republican party were to nominate a Roman Catholic candidate for President, they would hold the relatively small percentage of Republican voters who are Catholics. At the same time, they might stand to swing nearly half of all Democratic Catholics over to their ticket — or about one Democratic voter in seven.

Whichever party nominated a Catholic could probably count on substantial support from Catholic Independents — or a little over one fourth of all Independent voters in the nation. In early 1960, when Nixon was ahead of Kennedy on an overall basis (by 53 per cent to 47 per cent), Kennedy had the support of nearly two out of three Catholic Independents.

Who wins this electoral chess match? A precise answer is impossible, of course, without knowing just how stirred up the electorate might be on the religious issue by an actual campaign. Furthermore, the winner might well be decided not by the pro-Catholic but by the anti-Catholic vote. Some idea of what might happen, however, can be seen by a look at the behavior of Catholic voters in recent elections.

America's Catholic voters are centered largely in Northern metropolitan areas. Seven states have Catholic populations totaling more than one third of their entire population. Five of these (Rhode Island, Massachusetts, New Jersey, Connecticut and New Hampshire) are along the Eastern seaboard, one (Wisconsin) is in the Midwest, one (Louisiana) is in the South. Nearly six out of ten Catholic voters consider themselves Democrats in their basic party orientation — less than two in ten call themselves Republicans. In talking about the "Catholic vote," therefore, we are describing what is mainly a Northern Democrat bloc.

POLITICS OF CATHOLIC VOTERS

Consider themselves:

Democrats	58
Republicans	18
Independents	24

The support of this bloc has been crucial to Democratic election victories in recent years. When the Democrats have held the Catholic vote solidly in line, they have tended to win elections. In 1952, however, the Catholic voters, particularly sensitive to the Korean and Communist issues, broke sharply toward the Eisenhower-Nixon ticket. Again in 1956, when nearly half of all Catholics voted for Eisenhower, the Democrats could not find enough votes elsewhere to offset this loss.

VOTE OF CATHOLICS
1952-1958

	Democratic	Republican
1952 Presidential	56	44
1954 Congressional	69	31
1956 Presidential	51	49
1958 Congressional	75	25

In the 1958 Congressional elections, Catholic voters returned to the Democratic fold with three out of four voting for that party's candidates. It was with the strange political bedfellowship of these Northern Catholics and the Southern Protestants that the Democrats fashioned the combination of votes which gave the GOP such a crushing defeat at the polls in 1958.

Looked at region by region, the importance of the Catholic vote to the Democrats in 1958 becomes even more apparent. About four out of ten of the 39 million Catholics in the nation live in the twelve New England and Middle Atlantic states. Among Eastern Democrats, Catholics actually outnumbered Protestants in 1958. The heavily Democratic Catholic vote more than offset the heavily Republican vote of Protestants. In only the fourth

VOTE IN EASTERN STATES

1958 Congressional Elections

	All Voters	Catholic Voters	Protestant Voters
Democratic	53	68	36
Republican	47	32	64

election since 1896 in which they polled a comfortable majority of the Eastern vote, the Democrats won 72 out of a possible 129 seats at stake in that area from the House of Representatives.

In the traditional GOP stronghold of the Midwest in 1958, Catholic voters, although proportionately fewer in number than in the Eastern states, played a key role in tipping the scales in favor of the Democrats in the popular vote. The Republicans must normally capture about 90 seats in the Midwestern states if they hope to make up the seats they spot the Democrats in the South. In 1958,

VOTE IN MIDWESTERN STATES

1958 Congressional Elections

	All Voters	Catholic Voters	Protestant Voters
Democratic	53	76	48
Republican	47	24	52

slightly over half of Midwestern Protestants voted Republican, but with three out of four Midwestern Catholics voting Democratic, the end result was a Democratic majority in the popular vote and only 61 of the needed 90 seats going to the GOP.

In the Mountain and Pacific states, majorities of both Catholic and Protestant voters went Democratic in the 1958 elections. Counting the seat they picked up in Alaska, the Democrats took 32 out of 58 House seats at stake in those regions. The Catholic vote spelled the difference between a safe Democratic margin and a landslide, as the Far Western states went as heavily Democratic as they had since early New Deal days.

VOTE IN FAR WESTERN STATES
1958 Congressional Elections

	All Voters	*Catholic Voters*	*Protestant Voters*
Democratic	57	69	54
Republican	43	31	46

When the 111 House seats from the predominantly Protestant South were added to the Democratic total outside the South, they had one of the biggest majorities they have ever held in Congress. Even in the South, the small minority of Catholics there turned in a heavily Democratic vote — heavier, in fact, than the Protestant Democratic vote.

VOTE IN SOUTHERN STATES
1958 Congressional Elections

	All Voters	*Catholic Voters*	*Protestant Voters*
Democratic	80	83	71
Republican	20	17	29

In all, the Democrats won 172 seats in the 86th Congress from the states outside the South — or just over half of the 316 seats at stake in those areas. Trying to estimate a seat division from the division of the popular vote is, at best, a risky business. But calculating roughly, it seems likely that the Catholic vote outside of the South helped to give the Democrats anywhere from 25 to 40 additional seats. Without the Catholic vote, or had Catholics voted exactly as Protestants did, the Democrats might still have controlled the 86th Congress, but with a far smaller seat margin than they actually had.

The religious breakdown demonstrates that with heavy majorities of the Catholic vote going against them the Republicans can hardly hope to win a national election — unless some other factor disturbs the traditional political alignments. Obviously one such factor would be the votes that the GOP might stand to pick up from normally Democratic Protestants, particularly in the South, if the Democrats had a Catholic at the head of their ticket.

Under such circumstances, could the Northern Catholics offset the Southern defection from the Democratic ticket because of the South's objection to a Catholic? Which is more politically powerful — the *pro* or *anti* Catholic vote?

The full extent of both the Protestant and the Catholic reaction to a Catholic Presidential candidate obviously could not be measured until the final weeks or days of a political campaign. The degree to which the religious issue itself entered the campaign, the influence of other issues which might arise, the personality of the candidates — all are factors which might affect the final decision.

211

But some idea of how the religious issue might change the political picture can be gained from an analysis of Gallup Poll results.

In this analysis, the *known* degree of anti-Catholicism (those voters who say they would not vote for a Catholic) was measured against the *known* degree of pro-Catholicism (those Catholics who said they might vote for a Catholic on the opposition ticket).

In the spring of 1959, Senator Kennedy ran ahead of Vice-President Nixon by a substantial majority in a Gallup Poll trial test where the religion of the candidates was not called to the attention of voters.* Kennedy's majority was about the size of that polled by President Eisenhower in his 1956 election victory — Kennedy had 57 per cent, Nixon 43 per cent of all voters expressing a preference.

A companion finding mentioned earlier, however, showed that more than half of those interviewed did not know that Kennedy was a Roman Catholic. Yet obviously if Kennedy were nominated, his religion would be known by the vast majority of the electorate by Election Day. In trying to take into account this factor, some statistical sleight of hand produced some significant findings.

We first deducted from the Kennedy column all of those voters who said (elsewhere in the questionnaire) that they would not support a Catholic, and counted them for Nixon. This changed the race sharply — from a Democratic lead down to a dead-even contest. Clearly

*The question asked of all voters read as follows: "Suppose the presidential election were being held today. If John Kennedy were the Democratic candidate and Richard Nixon were the Republican candidate, which would you like to see win?"

212

IMPACT OF CATHOLIC ISSUE

Kennedy vs. Nixon — May, 1959

	All Voters	*Deducting Anti-Catholic Vote*	*Adding Catholic "Switch" Voters*
Kennedy	57	50	53
Nixon	43	50	47

the anti-Catholic vote was of a degree to seriously hurt a Catholic candidate. As a further step, we took away from Nixon all of his Catholic voters who said they might consider switching to a Catholic on the other ticket, and counted them for Kennedy. The lead then swung back to the Massachusetts Senator, but with a smaller margin than he had originally — 53 per cent compared to 57 per cent.

This kind of analysis assumes, of course, that all of those voters who oppose a Catholic would actually get to the polls and vote for his rival. For several reasons this may not happen. One is the tendency of the anti-Catholic sentiment to come from groups with a general low turnout. Another might be because of the candidates involved. Certain Southerners, for example, are in the position typified by one Virginia man's comment to a Gallup Poll reporter: "Well, I wouldn't like to see a Catholic. But I'd rather have a Catholic than I would have Nixon." By the same token, it is by no means certain that all Catholics who said they *might* vote for a fellow Catholic on the rival ticket would actually feel strongly enough about this on Election Day to make the switch.

213

Subsequent Gallup Polls, however, indicated that as political activity increased and a greater number of voters came to know Kennedy was a Catholic, some of these counteracting influences were beginning to play a role. During the fall and late winter of 1959, Kennedy was pulling an increasing number of Catholic Republicans away from Nixon. During this same period Nixon gained some ground from Protestant Democrats.

RELIGIOUS ISSUE AT WORK?
Nixon vs. Kennedy

	September, 1959	January, 1960
Kennedy's Vote from:		
Catholic Republicans	22	27
Nixon's Vote from:		
Protestant Democrats	28	31

By the time of the first 1960 primary elections, the religious issue seemed to be working in Kennedy's favor. He had been trailing Nixon nationally in Gallup Poll tests during the fall and winter of 1959. This was due in large part to the political boost that the Vice-President got when he stood up to Khrushchev in a widely televised debate at the American exhibition in Moscow. It was further motivated, once Nixon had returned from Russia in the late summer of 1959, by the fact of voters somehow associating Nixon's efforts with the President's new course of personal diplomacy. (It may go down as a political irony that the one time that the President was able to do the most for his party was during a time when many observers predicted that his influence would be the lowest.)

The returns from Wisconsin made clear, however, that a number of Catholic Republicans were attracted to Kennedy. As an increasing number of Catholic voters in Gallup Poll nationwide tests swung to Kennedy, he pulled up even with and then out ahead of the Vice-President.

In the final analysis, the full impact of the religious issue on a Presidential campaign may be determined by how much the chicken-and-egg factor is at work. Just how many Catholics decide that they should vote "Catholic" regardless of party may depend on how much anti-Catholicism is evident to them. And the number of Protestants who get out and vote against a Catholic may be determined by the extent to which it seems that Catholics are voting as a bloc for a candidate of their faith.

Some may feel that published poll results about the religious issue may tend to increase the possibility of *religious voting*. Perhaps this is so, but all the evidence is that polls have rarely influenced many votes; they have merely measured them. And whenever the Gallup Poll has published results dealing with the religious issue, the mail from readers has been unusually heavy. Complaints come in from Catholic readers who say this only stirs up a "non-existent issue." At the other extreme are letters from readers who dispute the results because they do not show that "every Protestant in this country is against a Catholic in the White House."

When Senator Kennedy spoke before the American Society of Newspaper Editors in the spring of 1960, he made the point that if there was bigotry enough to keep a Catholic out of the White House "then we ought to know it." If for no other reason, this has called for an impartial analysis of the whole religious issue.

12

The Sixties

As THE MIDDLE of the twentieth century drew near in 1949, a Gallup Poll asked the public for some of its predictions about the state of the world in the year 2000. Looking ahead fifty years, the people were optimistic on several counts. They believed cancer would be cured, they saw atomic energy being put to peaceful uses. But only fifteen Americans in every hundred thought that man would be on the moon by the end of the twentieth century. Ten years later, in the early part of 1960, another Gallup Poll found that just over half of Americans were confident that man would have landed on the moon by 1980.

If nothing else, this change emphasizes the risk in trying to predict the course of public opinion. We pollsters have had enough trouble trying to worry about how many voters might change their minds in the relatively few hours we have between the time the last pre-election interview is made and the moment the first voter actually enters the polling booth on Election Day.

But the electorate's behavior in recent years does suggest at least two things which will probably continue to be
true about the American political scene during the 1960s.

First, it seems likely that the voters will continue to
make up their minds on whom they want for President
largely on the basis of a candidate's personality rather
than his party. Both FDR and Eisenhower influenced
this pattern; it is one of their legacies to the politics of the
future.

Second, we can expect to see the continued dominance
of the Democratic party at the level of basic party
strength. The Democrats will probably continue to win
more congressional elections than the Republicans, no
matter which party the voters choose to put in the White
House.

To get what they wanted in the way of a Chief Executive in recent years, millions of Americans were ready and
willing to ignore political traditions. When they sensed
in Eisenhower what they felt were leadership qualities,
they voted for him and paid little heed to the fact that he
was allied with a political philosophy many of them rejected.

Most Americans, a Gallup Poll indicates, at least like
to *think* that they vote for the man and not his party. This
is true of majorities in both political parties. There is
frequently pride in the voice of a voter when he tells you
that *he* votes for the man — even though he may have
been a straight ticket voter all of his adult life.

The second likely political fact of the '60s — the Democratic party's superiority — is in many ways itself attribut-

able to the impact of a personality, Franklin D. Roosevelt. A great depression and a world war helped to establish the present party line-ups. But FDR's personality got stamped on the Democratic party and this sold the party to millions of voters on a long-term basis.

It is revealing that the one man who could ever defeat Eisenhower in Gallop Poll tests — once Ike had come into the full glare of the national political spotlight — was Roosevelt. In the summer of 1955, at a time when Eisenhower's popularity was the highest it had been up to that point, the Gallup Poll asked voters to make a choice in an intriguing hypothetical contest between these two greatest vote-getters of all time (FDR polled nearly 28 million votes in 1936, Ike got over 35 million in 1956). Roosevelt won the novel test by a substantial margin — by about the same percentage, in fact, that Eisenhower had over Stevenson in the 1952 election.

Aside from the posthumousness of the situation, there was another unrealistic aspect to this test. In death, Roosevelt undoubtedly came to be revered by many who might not have supported him during his lifetime. But it does seem eloquent testimony to the enormous personal appeal of the two men that such an "iffy" question left only one voter in twenty in the undecided column.

What these two aspects of the political picture may mean, of course, is that we will see more of the kind of divided government which has been in existence during eight of the past fifteen years — from 1946 to 1948 under Truman, from 1954 to 1960 under Eisenhower. If there is divided government, however, voters will probably be

219

little bothered. At least in 1959 only a minority of the American electorate said that it thought a President of one party and a Congress controlled by another was a bad thing — most people appeared either satisfied with or indifferent to the arrangement.

There seem to be really few things which could occur to drastically change the present party alignments. Another great depression would probably just make more Democrats. And it is doubtful if continued prosperity will make many more Republicans — at least it hasn't worked that way during the eight years of the Eisenhower administration. Another Korea might again make people mad at the President. But the original Korea didn't make that much of a difference in the party line-ups — when it was over there were still more Democrats than Republicans in the electorate; this has been true actually at least as far back as 1940.

The threat of nuclear war will probably continue the tendency in Presidential elections to vote for the man rather than the party. The voters will continue to want a man whose personality inspires their confidence and calms their fears. And it is generally true that when the American people have wanted something badly enough, they have somehow managed to get it in the long run.